THE
CHURCH
Needs
DELIVERANCE!

From The Prophetic Guard Series

BRANDIE N. GRAY

ISBN: 978-1-915930-25-5 PAPERBACK

ISBN: 978-1-915930-26-2 HARDBACK

ISBN: 978-1-915930-27-9 EBOOK

DEDICATION

This book is dedicated to the body of Christ, who loves Jesus' church and wants to see the church healthy and whole. Also, to those who are highly gifted spiritually and called by the Lord, yet are trying to find your place in today's church. I admonish you to stay strong in the Lord.

CONTENTS

INTRODUCTION

How did the church become this needy entity? The turning point for the church, I believe, came with the crucifixion of Apostle Paul, as the apostle of Jesus Christ was murdered. How did the spirit of murder enter the first-century church? How did it get access to the builders of the church? The answer is summed up in this scripture: *(John 8:44)*, Satan has been a murderer from the very beginning. The destruction of the Jewish Temple by the Roman Empire in 70 A.D. marked a multilayered dimensional change. The fall of the Temple gave way to the church we see today. Not the character of the church we see today just the construct of it.

Why this book, some may be asking. I can guarantee it was something I had no idea God would impart into me, but it is God's Spirit that is infused throughout this book. It is His wisdom and desire, solely inspired by Him and the things He allowed me to experience.

The title: *The Church Needs Deliverance,* caught me by complete surprise when I heard it within my inner being. After hearing the title, this is what was spoken to me by Holy Spirit, "they get away with it because where there are two or three gathered in Jesus' name, He is in the midst of them. That is a guarantee from God." Most false church leaders know this, and they bank on this promise from God. If there is an assembling or gathering of 1,000 souls and 998 are not saved, some may be into mixture with darkness, or there may be some sordid individuals or workers of iniquity the bible calls them, in that 998 people out of 1000. With this, all it takes is the two or three to be gathered in His name, and Jesus promises to be right in the midst of all the others, just for those two or three who represent Him. If I am a false church leader sent by Satan, I will take those odds of looking like the real church.

I prayed and asked the Lord, why does His church need deliverance? The answer was, "because they that lead it have mishandled the divine protocol needed to run it." I think it is safe to insert here that this isn't about every church. I will say this a few times throughout this book. Moreover, the leaders are missing Him, Jesus. Some of the leaders of the church have gone away from first being totally sold out to Jesus. Second, they have gone away from biblically sound doctrine, and lastly, not allowing Holy Spirit His portion of work within the congregation.

Holy Spirit is a worker, He comes on the scene to get a specific job done, and He is sent by the Father. Holy Spirit is Jesus' Spirit allotted to move upon the earth. The thing about Holy Spirit is, He is like the wind, you do not know which direction He is going to move. Being totally yielded to Holy Spirit means you are on His timetable, not the congregations. At times, most church leaders move on their own time, thus quenching the move of the Holy Spirit. When Holy Spirit is quenched, He is unable to continue to do the will or work of the Father. The same way Jesus told His disciples, "I can only do what I see my Father, who sent Me, do. The same with Holy Spirit, He is Jesus' Spirit. We grieve Holy Spirit by quenching His working ability in the earth. This is the cause for an automatic need for deliverance in the church.

I have recently heard some in ministry preach they want a move of God. So, you pray for them to see a move of God within their midst. The move starts like a little spark to a flame. The move of God hits the least of these. It didn't start at the head like the minister wanted. After the smallest spark was set, the minister moved away from the move. Thus, quenching Holy Spirit, which caused grief in Him. He came to give the minister what they have been asking for and because it didn't look the way the minister wanted the move to look or it was not done in a manner they thought it should, which was just the beginning of what God planned, they moved away from expressing the desire for a move of God. This church needs deliverance!

Many church leaders and those that grew up in the church can't quite grasp how God would pull an individual out of the church. They have done church for so long that they can't see why God would pull certain people away from the house of prayer for a season. This book is a part of that season. I never grew up in the church like some. When I did go, God would start dealing with me about His church. The Lord opened my eyes on many occasions in many services. I was having open visions of what goes on behind the scenes in the church and God began to visually display to me the areas of the church in which He hasn't been pleased for a very long time. I never entered these places looking for anything wrong or finding fault. I would always go looking to praise the Lord and I did.

Since being saved, God has allowed me to see an individual's heart through His lenses. This allows me to always see them as good, in the beginning. When the ugly would show up in them, it perplexed me because I thought they were deeply a genuine person or people. With the church, it was extremely perplexing because what I saw spiritually did not align with what was happening in the natural. It was such a contrast between personality and character. I asked God, "what is this I'm experiencing within the construct of the church?" because I have never been to the four walls of the church and felt the love of Jesus amongst the people I was worshipping with. I would see the people in the church so differently because I was seeing them through the lens of God. I hurt for the current church because there are so many things God wants to do through her. Yet, she continues to ignore Him. She has strayed from her first love to remain the prostitute of the world.

It is in this book that I plan to highlight just what God visually displayed to me about His house in which He isn't pleased with. Over the last decade I've had this burden of wanting the people of God to handle the house of God with great care. I've longed to see the people of God serious about the things of God. The burden has been so strong to experience love in the church. The burden of God has clasped me down so intensely, that I cannot get away from its hold until God releases me. I was birthed into this burden, God placed it within me. He is in agony over us His church. God views us as He did the children of Israel. Anywhere you see the children of Israel written in the bible, God said, "just plug the name church there because they are the same through His eyes."

Yet, I am burdened still, to see God's true power in love on display in the house of God. Burdened the more to see the church flow in the greater works. Burdened to see the church finally step away from her pimp, the world. Strongly burdened to see and hear what the true voice of the church sounds like. Again, burdened to see the church in her kingdom role here on the earth. Finally, burdened to see the church free from witchcraft and rebellion.

Therefore, God started dealing with me about the Bride He created for Christ. And she needs deliverance!

CHAPTER 1

THE CHURCH AND THE WORLD

Over the years, I have observed that similar to the concerns or issues one may deal with in the world, you will deal with those same concerns or issues in some churches, to a degree. Particularly, everyone isn't saved on the same level, including the pew and the pulpit. You can simulate this understanding via the current American school system. For example, at the beginning of the school year, pick a grade level. You have students starting a class at the same time on the same day, showing up every day, and completing the same work and/or assignments. However, by the last day of school, some students learned more or less than others. Why didn't each student learn on the same exact level? Why is it that multiple students can retain more information than others in a typical school year?

So be it with our salvation and spiritual maturation, which are synonymous with the public school system of the United States and the church system. From this approach, we can presume that those different grades afford specific learning and exposure; as students advance in learning, they progress to a higher grade. Similarly, the spirit realm isn't an endless plane but a realm of levels and cadre. Your current spiritual level of insight and eyes of your understanding being enlightened determines what you see, know, and understand via Holy Spirit. This insight that the divine impartation of activating one spiritual gift's needs a tutor and a governor that is spoken of in Galatians 4:2 (KJV). This is where the teacher comes in, in the church, not just the church leadership, but from the Spirit of Truth, providing the understanding on how to govern and tutor those spiritually imparted through His Spirit, yielding our natural intellect to His all-knowing Spiritual intellect.

> "NOW I say, That the heir, as long as he is a child, differeth nothing from a servant, though he be lord of all; But is under tutors and governors until the time appointed of the father." (Galatians 4:1-2)

While growing up, I vividly remember having some excellent teachers who were exemplary both in and out of the classroom. Conversely, others were just there for the paycheck, which reflected in their teaching style or presentation. The kingdom of God is not different; some leaders/teachers of the gospel of Jesus Christ are diligent stewards, faithful shepherds, and wonderful teachers of spiritual truths and mysteries that help, equip, strengthen, establish, and mature believers in their walk with God. However, some leaders/teachers are not good teachers for a group of people, not because they are bad leaders, but because they may lack certain qualities that can hamper the growth of the group they teach. This becomes more dangerous if the group they teach have been called by God.

I started this chapter by explaining that we see the same people in the church as we see in the world and how the U.S. school system parallels the church's system. In the U.S. school system, 30 students can be lumped into a classroom, but multiple students may have multiple learning styles, where one group of students may flourish and grow. With several other students, the teaching style of the teacher may not be high enough and those students may become inattentive because the work and the teaching is too easy. You may have another set of students within the 30, that may not be able to grasp the same teaching that was too easy for the other students. It's the same for the church. So, to summate, there are various learning styles, and various speeds to learning also. Some learn differently than the general population and we must not lump people into a generalized learning style. And I get it, it costs resources to educate the right way, it also takes time to educate the right way! Something some are not willing to give up is their time or resources, putting in the necessary work.

Mostly, or in some church settings, we experience a deficiency of spiritual power. That is because some spiritual leaders/teachers may not be founded on a spiritual level of growth that can catapult the spiritual intellect of the highly gifted and anointed by God. This leader, he or she may be the right fit for the congregation they minister to, yet there are other individuals that may need a higher grade level of the anointing.

Furthermore, I guarantee that if we just took the time out to properly educate, we would find out that we are amongst more gifted geniuses than we thought, even the ones whom God has highly gifted in the Spirit for His Kingdom. It is not unusual to see believers who require special spiritual attention because they have a higher spiritual intellect and intelligence. Whoever leads these special traits in believers must be helped by God and gifted with special abilities to manage their extraordinary need for a gifted tutor or governor. Otherwise, the teacher may be good for the congregation, yet starve others with special spiritual needs and rapid spiritual growth.

The Apostle Paul's Growth Pattern

> But when it pleased God, who separated me from my mother's womb, and called me by his grace, to reveal his Son in me, that I might preach him among the heathen; immediately I conferred not with flesh and blood: neither went I up to Jerusalem to them which were apostles before me; but I went into Arabia and returned again unto Damascus. Then after three years I went up to Jerusalem to see Peter, and abode with him fifteen days.
> (Galatians. 1:15-18)

Apostle Paul was an example of a believer with exemplary spiritual needs. Before his conversion, he was a renowned intellectual and highly influential person. After his encounter with Jesus, he was led to the wilderness of Arabia where he underwent discipleship training for three (3) years, not under any man, but Jesus. Therefore, in His infinite wisdom, God knew that it would be difficult for a man to disciple Apostle Paul in that season of Paul's life. To prevent any gap or error in his spiritual growth, Jesus became Paul's teacher and instructor. Biblically, we don't read much of Paul's tutelage in

Arabia, but I can imagine it was a rigorous course study. Apostle Paul, once released by Jesus to go into Jerusalem, was extended the right hand of fellowship by those Apostles that were the pillars in which the first-century church stood upon. Jesus' ministry was three years, and Paul's course in ministry and action was three years before his meet-up with Peter in the book of Acts.

Before becoming Apostle Paul, Saul had to go to Arabia because what he was about to embark on took another type of sight. A keener spiritual clarity. Saul, being a biblical scholar from his youth, already had vision for the law. But Jesus wanted to open his sight to the New Covenant and cause, now Paul, to be a converter to the Gentiles. So, Saul's old view had to be darkened. And Jesus did just that for three days. Jesus darkened Saul's old vision.

"And Saul, yet breathing out threatenings and slaughter against the disciples of the Lord, went unto the high priest, And desired of him letters to Damascus to the synagogues, that if he found any of this way, whether they were men or women, he might bring them bound unto Jerusalem." And as he journeyed, he came near Damascus: and suddenly there shined round about him a light from heaven: And he fell to the earth, and heard a voice saying unto him, Saul, Saul, why persecutest thou me? And he said, Who art thou, Lord? And the Lord said, I am Jesus whom thou persecutest: it is hard for thee to kick against the pricks." (Acts 9:1-5)

"And he trembling and astonished said, Lord, what wilt thou have me to do? And the Lord said unto him, Arise, and go into the city, and it shall be told thee what thou must do. And the men which journeyed with him stood

> speechless, hearing a voice, but seeing no man. And Saul arose from the earth; and when his eyes were opened, he saw no man: but they led him by the hand, and brought him into Damascus. And he was three days without sight, and neither did eat nor drink." (Acts 9:6-9)

Try to picture having Ananias, Sapphira, Jonah, Reuben, and Apostle Paul in a Sunday School class, under the leadership of an average leader. In no distant time, Sunday School lessons that ought to bless the class would turn into a mini civil war, because Apostle Paul would ask complex and compiled questions. The teacher, in a bit to save his or her face, may dodge or want to shut him up. Alas! The fiery nature of Apostle Paul would resist such a teacher, and the outcome may be unpredictable.

If Apostle Paul rebuked the hypocrisy of Apostle Peter, had a sharp disagreement with Barnabas, rejected Mark, and called the Galatians "foolish", much more would he do to any heretic preacher or any unscriptural dogma predicated by the church.

God saw Saul's extraordinary spiritual needs before they posed any challenge; therefore, He singled him out for a unique teaching and training program that lasted three (3) years. Does the church have an "Arabia wilderness" platform for Christians with these unique mantles and metrons? I can answer that from experience and say no, that most churches don't. Thus, without these much-needed platforms, this absence can stagnate, stall, or stunt a believers spiritual growth when you lump those with unique mantles or extraordinary spiritual needs like the Apostle Paul into the general population's learning style.

CHAPTER 2

THE CHURCH?

A few years ago, I had the awesome privilege of attending a conference to divinely impart my spiritual gifts. My gifts were stirred all the way up on ten, and I was exceptionally equipped for godly service. I was on fire for God and honestly, every room that I entered since the impartation of my gifts could sense it too, meaning that everyone I was around from that point on, knew something was different about me. I was charged for the kingdom of God. But soon after that initial born-again, baptized-in-fire experience, I hit a rough patch in ministry called the church system. This system can consist of groups of tight-knit clicks that prevent the entrance of newcomers with true power from God. They have their molds, and you get kicked to the curb if you don't fit into those molds. Mandatorily, you must come up through their ranks and systems before you can be authenticated as being called by God. Bless the Lord if you are still on fire by the time they are done authenticating you!

Do not be called by Holy Spirit and not them! The man-made doctrine pushers, and/or false leaders or teachers will call Holy Spirit a liar, just so you won't walk in the call God has placed on your life. In some churches they will try and make you out to be a total heathen, witch, sorcerer, rogue believer, vagabond, or a spiritual bastard, which is the lack of spiritual parents, diminishing and attempting to demonize your spiritual gifts, thus also attempting to cause you not to bear fruit for the kingdom, where Father has anointed you to do so. But guess what? For one that is a novice in the things of God, the church, and/or the spirit realm, these accusations will have you reeling. As well, they should have you reeling, causing you to be stunned, shocked, or even confused.

That is the plot of the enemy, to throw you off the course of using your spiritual giftings. With all these negative words spoken, we can only question, do we have the same Holy Spirit? But this is what Satan wants, that seed of your spiritual gifts to fall along the wayside, to be trodden underfoot, to be plucked up by birds, or choked out by thorns and thistles, all before the Holy Spirit can use you. This is a device that the adversary uses against the new believer. Even Jesus!

Even Jesus

"For John the Baptist came neither eating bread nor drinking wine; and ye say, he hath a devil. The Son of man is come eating and drinking; and ye say, behold a gluttonous man, and a winebibber, a friend of publicans and sinners!" (Luke 7:33-34)

Even Jesus, the author, and finisher of our faith was screened and weighed by these "churchy" evaluators. They found him unworthy because he did not fit into their molds. They queried John the Baptist for not eating bread nor drinking wine and slammed Jesus for taking excess bread. Interestingly, they hallow the Sabbath more than the Creator of the Sabbath – questioning why Jesus healed the sick on the Sabbath day. Having observed their characters, Jesus branded them with a proper name – "hypocrites!" From the text, it is safe to mention that some that have mounted the church pulpits could possibly be operating in hypocrisy, especially when they despise a new convert, and their true baptism in Holy Spirit, whom He, the Holy Spirit, now can operate through.

> "But woe unto you, scribes and Pharisees, hypocrites! for ye shut up the kingdom of heaven against men: for ye neither go in yourselves, neither suffer ye them that are entering to go in." (Matthew 23:13)

> "And He spake this parable unto certain which trusted in themselves that they were righteous, and despised others: Two men went up into the temple to pray; the one a Pharisee, and the other a publican. The Pharisee stood and prayed thus with himself, God, I thank Thee, that I am not as other men are, extortioners, unjust, adulterers, or even as this publican. I fast twice in the week, I give tithes of all that I possess. And the publican, standing afar off, would not lift up so much as his eyes unto heaven, but smote upon his breast, saying, God be merciful to me a sinner. I tell you, this man went down to his house justified rather than the other: for every one that exalteth himself shall be abased; and he that humbleth himself shall be exalted." (Luke 18:9-14)

These churchy evaluators are audacious enough to despise your ministerial call. If necessary, they could brand the Holy Spirit a liar – the scribes said Jesus possessed the spirit of Beelzebub. Their disillusioned view has limited God's way of calling people into ministry to a certain bandwidth. Quizzically, do we have the same Holy Spirit? I ask again. If I believe that you are called by God and have extended the hand of fellowship to you, why can't you believe God called me into His fold? It may be one or two things. Either you don't honestly know God, or you have inclined that I won't bow to the false church system.

Holy Spirit, How Do You See the Church System?

Let me say this before I go any further. There will be some that are already upset about this book from the title alone. Moreover, this book is referring to all churches, not just the ones I have ever visited or heard about. Also, if the book isn't for you, then, it isn't for you. Just take it as a leisure read. Also, I do not have anything against God's true church, for there is a true church and a false church. Just like there is good and evil, the same applies to the church system. In addition, I do have something against the mess-laden, busybody systems, hating to see someone come up without that system's hand of control, is what my problem is with the false church.

In this same system, I am alarmed by the unresisted open witchcraft and rebellion that is going on in the false church systems, the unending manipulation of people's minds, and the narcissistic behavior of some people in leadership positions. These are some brewing issues within the false church. In addition, this stronghold of title and position worship as if there is not enough room for someone else to have a position in the kingdom of God is a problem, especially in the false church. This is one of the meanings of Jesus saying, "you have the keys to the kingdom, you won't go in, but you won't allow anyone else to enter either."

I am paraphrasing Matthew 23:13 here, but it is true. Needless to add, the obsession with titles and positions as if these tags are criteria for entering the kingdom of God, is an error that the scribes and Pharisees made before the church and Jesus. When you look at the scribes and Pharisees, ask the question, what is the benefit of keeping the keys of the kingdom from people? Could one of the keys be a financial key? These types of practices remind us of a money-struck or money-hungry leader of a corporation. There seems not to be a clear demarcation between the church of God and earthly corporations as it relates to an undying passion for money and profit. Are we still in faith when we intentionally use God as a financial ladder to meet our selfish goals and aspirations?

An example of this could be seen biblically when we examine the character of Judas Iscariot. Being a disciple of Jesus Christ, Jesus knew that Judas was stealing from the money bag. However, Judas' unwillingness to purify his heart concerning his theft of the kingdom, ultimately destroyed him in the end. Now Judas, having numbed his conscience against the warnings of the Holy Spirit and not having a clear boundary between God's desire for the money received and Judas' own personal cravings for money and possessions (greed), can we boldly say that we still have faith when our desire, in greed, outweighs God's desire for His church? Are these in ministry (the false church) that, only using the ministry for personal gain, greed, and/or pride of life? These things were taking place when Jesus walked the earth:

> "And Jesus went into the temple of God, and cast out all them that sold and bought in the temple, and overthrew the tables of the moneychangers, and the seats of them that sold doves, And said unto them, It is written, My house shall be called the house of prayer; but ye have made it a den of thieves." (Matthew 21:12-13)

The Holy Spirit sees these types of churches or ministries as a quencher of His will, and it grieves Him greatly and is very troubling to my spirit as well.

Church Expectations and Realizations

Having realized that someone is holding a kingdom key that opens my next move that can help advance the kingdom of God, spurs holy joy and excitement in me because at this point, I am divinely equipped for service, and gifted – I have been given the word from the Lord! I am ready to get into the trenches and the hills with my key holders. We are about to take the world by storm, turning it upside down for God. I have been divinely imparted to operate in the gifts given to the church by Jesus, Holy Spirit, and God the Father. This experience is a game-changer! I am not talking about Christians who are ecstatic because they fellowship with people whose perception of God's presence is measured by the tune and vibe of music or other charismatic activities.

Instead, I'm referring to people on fire for the Lord, whose lives create an atmosphere of miracles, signs, and wonders because we believe God. Fellowshipping with brethren who are on fire for God is nothing short of a wonder. It is imperative when assembling, that we stay hot and on fire for God because we would not be offering Him the type of praise that He desires. Being baptized in the Holy Spirit opens you up to the move of the Spirit of God and enhances your spiritual sensitivity when we assemble. Therefore, Jesus requests that we are filled with His Spirit. Unless we are born again by the water and Spirit, we cannot see the Kingdom of God.

"Jesus answered, Verily, verily, I say unto thee, Except a man be born of water and of the Spirit, he cannot enter into the kingdom of God." (John 3:5)

During corporate worship, realizing that you praise God amongst brethren who are equally on fire for the Lord is an exhilarating experience. A person endowed with the spirit of discernment can easily pick up on the spirit of other believers – thank God for the Holy Spirit. The ability to discern helped Jesus in his earthly ministry, helping Him to answer the critical questions of who, when, where, and what to do and the right time to do them.

After becoming a believer, something I thought, was that discernment would help me recognize my spiritual tribe, as some would call it. For instance, you should be able to look around and affirmatively say that these people dance, praise, and honor God like me. I am divinely imparted by the Holy Spirit, I'm home, I'm comfortable, and I fit in here.

Later, I learned I was spiritually immature, and God had another plan for me. What I was experiencing at this time could be likened to one being on top of a body of water in a boat but lacking the ability to see the forceful undercurrents turning that gathering of believers. I could not see the enemy's stirring of the great shout, music, and other energetic activities. As I began to spiritually mature, I learned that some of these activities were nothing more than sensationalism and emotionalism, as well as fitness routines. Yet, it is incredible to note that God will always honor Himself in these gatherings, simply because of His name, love, and the presence of genuine worshippers, regardless of how few there are.

> "For where two or three are gathered together in my name, there am I in the midst of them." (Matthew 18:20)

So, when the Holy Spirit comes into the room or assembly, the spiritual impartation begins. He starts moving on the face of the gathering just like He moved on the face of the deep in the beginning, in the book of Genesis. He is looking for His word in the sanctuary to perform it. When we keep His word in our hearts and maintain a lifestyle of love and holiness, the Holy Spirit will activate or impart our gifts.

However, when you are activated but young in the things of the Spirit, the enemy will try to manipulate your gifts. Through this scheme, he has thrown many people off the track of faith. The parable of the Sower, as narrated by Jesus, unveils several attacks launched against God's Word as soon as it is planted in the heart of a new convert.

> "Hear ye therefore the parable of the Sower. When any one heareth the word of the kingdom, and understandeth it not, then cometh the wicked one, and catcheth away that which was sown in his heart. This is he which received seed by the wayside. But he that received the seed into stony places, the same is he that heareth the word, and anon with joy receiveth it; yet hath he not root in himself, but dureth for a while: for when tribulation or persecution ariseth because of the word, by and by he is offended. He also that received seed among the thorns is he that heareth the word; and the care of this world, and the deceitfulness of riches, choke the word, and he becometh unfruitful." (Matthew 13:18-22)

CHAPTER 3

THE SAME SYSTEM THAT ACTIVATED YOU DOES NOT WANT YOU

What do you see as you look out over the landscape of the church system? Well, it is important to note that my viewpoint is not the opinion of everyone, but this is what the Holy Spirit allowed me to see. It's glaring that in any system of the world, there are usually flaws and possible breakups. Interestingly, the Holy Spirit is certainly concerned about the system God holds so dear to His heart, which is the church. A function of the Holy Spirit is the work of equipping and caring for the church of God, which Jesus calls the house of prayer.

> Howbeit when He, the Spirit of truth, is come, He will guide you into all truth: for He shall not speak of Himself; but whatsoever He shall hear, that shall He speak: and He will show you things to come. He shall glorify Me: for He shall receive of Mine, and shall show it unto you. All things that the Father hath are Mine: therefore said I, that He shall take of Mine, and shall show it unto you (John 16:13-15).

When Jesus ascended to the Father, He left His disciples in charge of building a system that would turn the world upside down. He told them plainly, *"Verily, verily, I say unto you, He that believeth on Me, the works that I do shall he also do; and greater works than these shall he do, because I go unto my Father."* **(John. 14:12)**

This does not only connote magnitude, but it also demonstrates span and spread. We can also honestly notate, that turning the world upside down isn't and wasn't a one-time flipping or turning. This type of commission from Jesus is a daily turning. This is because the adversary, Satan, is a relentless being. Satan is ancient and full of schemes to come against the church, the saints, and anything that resembles holiness. So, the church that Christ left to be built by His Apostles will constantly receive violence towards it, just do not let the violent take it by force. The turning upside down is a constant as well. If we are not flipping and turning the world upside down constantly, would you agree, "The Church Needs Deliverance?" So, we should be even more relentless, above the adversary in the greater works and holiness, thus advancing the kingdom of God.

As we strive to fulfill this mandate, the Holy Spirit is concerned about how we treat His house of prayer. It is not just the house (physical structure) that matters in God's desire for humanity, but the individuals He dwells in spiritually. It is necessary to let you know that believers in Christ are the most delicate people to maltreat on earth. Why? They have divine support. Anyone that touches them touches the apple of God's eye, those that are His because He redeemed them with Jesus' precious blood.

> "Know ye not that ye are the temple of God, and that the Spirit of God dwelleth in you? If any man defile the temple of God, him shall God destroy; for the temple of God is holy, which temple ye are." (1 Corinthians 3:16-17)

Obligate as Holy Spirit Imparts

God is the wisest planner, and He knew His plan for each of us before we were formed in the womb. He detests emptiness and vainness, so He created everything for a purpose and time as Ecclesiastes 3:1 explains, "To everything, there is a season and a time to every purpose under heaven."   The very nature of God, how He creates, brings forth and has a structure to everything He does, allows us to understand that when you activate and/or impart the gifts of His people without an active plan on when, where, or how to use these spiritual gifts, you can either be setting some believers up for church hurt, frustration, or spiritual negligence.

The reason for this negligence is not far-fetched. Experience shows that abandonment tends to drain the power of a charged battery within a short time. Another example is the rate at which idle tools lose their potency and relevance. In this kingdom, every regenerated soul is of kingdom use, and not a spectator. Therefore, you need to allow the people of God to shine in grace and glory as God has called them forth. Any unused sharp object will constitute a danger in its environment. Activation or impartation will put a new heart, spirit, and unquenchable zeal in a converted soul. And if anyone's impartation and new identity in God is as aggressive as mine, such an individual will become unstoppable.

There is a need to create an enabling environment for growth and development in the body. There is no need to impart or activate people if you are not ready to see their full expression of spiritual maturation. For instance, when Stephen was chosen to serve the tables in Acts 6, he was humanly ordained as a deacon. But he suddenly grew to become a powerful preacher with signs and wonders following him like the apostles. He did not stop there; he manifested grace till he became the first Christian martyr to be welcomed with a heavenly ovation into glory in Acts 7.

If Stephen was restricted by those around him or by the apostles, there's no doubt there would have been a problem. Today, it is evident that there are some spiritually wounded (but imparted) believers walking around, that have been restricted by those in leadership. Some of their wounds are caused by compression and choking within their domains. Other wounds can be caused by a demonic spirit of rejection inside and outside of the body (the church), which is a constant tactic used by the enemy to make you feel unworthy to be used by God, attempting to quench who you are in Christ and how you are to be used for His kingdom (your kingdom assignment). I just pray that the same individuals that were rejected by man, did not and would not give up on Jesus and His will and desire for their lives. Even when you feel like everyone else has given up on you or has rejected you, Jesus would never give up on you or reject you. His own blood that was shed for each of us, tells us this truth. Jesus loves you and has a purpose for you!

The machine as the church allegory

I want you to look carefully at the church as a machine with various moving parts without any room for modification or a need for overhauling. Is the machine bad at this moment, or is it running smoothly with new parts? Perhaps you believe it doesn't need new parts because it's been moving so well for years. This machine has "self-calibration" with built-in quality control and a "self-repair" mechanism or a built-in air conditioner. But the rigid church system will fight tooth and nail, claiming that there is no need to change the parts, no need for overhauling; "if it is not physically broken, (by the untrained sight) why fix it?" Unknown to them, it is never the plan of God to see His church breakdown. Hence, He will always send new parts to uphold and upgrade the system, even when it is not popular.

Picture this, would not Saul/Apostle Paul have been a brand new, unpopular, rejected, replacement part after his road to Damascus experience? If you look at Saul before his Damascus experience, he was a persecutor of Christians. During his road to Damascus and Arabia Wilderness experience, becoming Apostle Paul, he was blinded for 3 days and after 3 days and 3 years, given a new way to see and a new way of bringing the Gentiles into the fold by God, through Jesus Christ.

If God did not add Apostle Paul as a brand new shinney part to the machine (the church), the Gentiles, in number, would not have received the same salvation offered to the Jews through Jesus Christ. God being God would have found a way. Nonetheless, Apostle Paul is a wonderful example of using individuals (adding new parts) in the body (the church as a machine) in a new way, to advance the kingdom of God.

This machine (the church) has a Holy handler (God), who sits high and looks low. In fact, this handler sees

His creation afar off, yet holds them dear to His heart. He knows the end from the beginning. So, God sees what His church needs but the holders of the keys are at times blind to it, just as the scribes and Pharisees were. Without delay, God gives the new part the clearance to replace the old part. But the old machine will not accept the new part/feature unless the pieces fit in the way the machine wants them to. Oh! The machine has forgotten its Creator, not remembering that its Creator has all the parts and makes the engine run.

What do we do with the parts that the machine doesn't tolerate?

Be informed that these new parts are not cheap to manufacture. They are premium divine tools in God's arsenal, yet rejected by men. What will God do with the old machine (traditional church system) that will not adopt His new device (movement)? This analysis represents Jesus' walk on the earth. The old church couldn't receive the new dynamic moves that Jesus was making upon the earth.

Today, this sad tale repeats itself unabated – the old versus the new. When Jesus walked this earth, the rigid religious tradition of His time rose against Him. The scribes and Pharisees vehemently wrestled against Jesus' messages that were clearing off tradition and culture, inhibiting the people from knowing God. Every church leader must do a self-examination to know his/her status. You need to know the actual state of your mind and heart, whether you are erring or focusing on the cross. It is important to note that a burst with a spill is unavoidable whenever new wine is poured into old wineskins.

Unfortunately, the church mimics the world's leadership style. There are people in leadership positions in the body of Christ that God has relegated but refuse to step down. So then, why are we activating and imparting people we know are called to special positions in the body of Christ but denying them the required leadership support? Certain leaders have become controlling rulers and are unwilling to groom their successors. Their unscriptural leadership stance can only produce rebels or raise persons just as stubborn as they are.

Every King Saul must know that either by war or death, the emergence of King David, the one God chose, is inevitable. Interestingly, the pivotal role King Saul played was instrumental to the jaw-dropping feat of David. When the courageous words of David were narrated to Saul, he sent for him. This paved the way for David's impartation, putting him in the position to do what he was called to do.

> "And when the words were heard which David spake, they rehearsed them before Saul: and he sent for him."
> (1 Samuel 17:31)

King Saul built a bridge for David's victory, not a wall against it. After agreeing to David's quest to fight the uncircumcised Philistine, Goliath, Saul prayed and equipped David for victory. This is exemplary leadership.

> "And Saul armed David with his armor, and he put a helmet of brass upon his head; also he armed him with a coat of mail." (1 Samuel 17:38).

After killing Goliath, David's influence grew exponentially. His valiant act attracted the voluntary service of praise singers who sang his praise and hallowed his feat. Immediately, King Saul, the man who equipped David, could not tolerate him anymore. He became dissatisfied and uncomfortable because he did not have enough room in his heart to contain David's greatness.

Oh! This is a true picture of so many leaders in today's church. We urgently need to repent!

> "And it came to pass as they came, when David was returned from the slaughter of the Philistine, that the women came out of all cities of Israel, singing and dancing, to meet King Saul, with tabrets, with joy, and with instruments of music. And the women answered one another as they played, and said, Saul hath slain his thousands, and David his ten thousands. And Saul was very wroth, and the saying displeased him; and he said, they have ascribed unto David ten thousands, and to me they have ascribed but thousands: and what can he have more but the kingdom? And Saul eyed David from that day and forward." (1 Samuel 18:6-9)

God had rejected Saul, but he refused to leave his platform for the one God chose, David. He was ruling the people of God without the presence and support of God. This is likened to the current mindsets of some church leaders this very day.

> "And the Lord said unto Samuel, how long wilt thou mourn for Saul, seeing I have rejected him from reigning over Israel? Fill thine horn with oil, and go, I will send thee to Jesse the Bethlehemite: for I have provided Me a king among his sons." (1 Samuel 16:1)

You can't do the things of God right if you don't have the right relationship with Him. We are enjoined to serve God in Spirit and truth, simple! Saul tried to work for God in his own way but was rejected. Uzzah stepped out of God's ordinance, and he paid the price. Pharaoh denied the people of God the freedom to serve God, and he paid the ultimate price. Please, let the people under you grow and glow in the center of God's will. If you have lost contact with God, stop guiding people, resign from your leadership position, and refrain from handling the holy things of God.

CHAPTER 4

JESUS AS THE APPOINTER

When you give your totality to Jesus Christ, your spirit man wants to start running and getting things accomplished for the kingdom of God. Are you ready for the real you, your new and true identity in Christ, after you have been born again and baptized in the Holy Spirit? The better question is, is your local assembly properly equipped to steward and strengthen you to your full stature in Christ, where God has given you a kingdom assignment and gifts to aid in your kingdom assignment?

But, oh no, my newly spiritually imparted friend of God. You are now required to sit down, be quiet, and not move. Sit right here in this place, usually in the back, muzzled spiritually, and told not to move until told by men to go forth. You must be sent out from this specific church or from this specific denomination, from right here, the place where you are told to sit down, be quiet, and not move. Yet, some have had their road to Damascus encounter with Christ after their experience of being born again.

To the American church, it is impossible for someone to go into ministry the route of an Apostle Paul. Some church leaders in the body of Christ do not want you moving in ministry as the Apostle Paul introduced. In fact, some Christian leaders do not believe God can cause some to have that road to Damascus or Arabia experience today, though Apostle Paul's encounter with Jesus Christ sparked a new metron of ministry that the body of Christ and its leaders can examine and build upon in today's modern church.

So what did Saul/Apostle Paul's conversion really mean to the church and why do the false church leaders today hate that there is another way of going into ministry? Apostle Paul's conversion represented the beginning of a church planter or builder, without the initial need for anyone telling him he could plant churches, but first, he preached. The Bible says in Acts 9 once Ananias got word that Saul was Jesus' chosen vessel, Ananias went to Saul, laid his hands on Saul and immediately Saul regained his sight and Ananias baptized Saul. Saul then ate a meal that strengthened him for his next journey, but before he remained a couple of days in Damascus. Yet after that, the Bible says Saul, in Acts 9:20, immediately preached Christ in the synagogues:

"And there was a certain disciple at Damascus, named Ananias; and to him said the Lord in a vision, Ananias. And he said, Behold, I am here, Lord. And the Lord said unto him, Arise, and go into the street which is called Straight, and enquire in the house of Judas for one called Saul, of Tarsus: for, behold, he prayeth, And hath seen in a vision a man named Ananias coming in, and putting his hand on him, that he might receive his sight. Then Ananias answered, Lord, I have heard by many of this man, how much evil he hath done to thy saints at Jerusalem: And here he hath authority from the chief priests to bind all that call on thy name. (Acts 9:10-14)

"But the Lord said unto him, Go thy way: for he is a chosen vessel unto Me, to bear My name before the Gentiles, and kings, and the children of Israel: For I will shew him how great things he must suffer for My name's sake. And Ananias went his way, and entered into the house; and putting his hands on him said, Brother Saul, the Lord, even Jesus, that appeared unto thee in the way as thou camest, hath sent me, that thou mightiest receive thy sight, and be filled with the Holy Ghost. And immediately there fell from his eyes as it had been scales: and he received sight forthwith, and arose, and was baptized. And when he had received meat, he was strengthened. Then was Saul certain days with the disciples which were at Damascus. And straightway he preached Christ in the synagogues, that He is the Son of God." (Acts 9:14-20)

Wait, how did Saul go from being a super Pharisee of the law to becoming one who could preach on Christ, the Son of God? How did Saul learn of Jesus in a new covenant way so quickly? What did Ananias impart into him or better yet, what gift did the Holy Spirit impart once Saul was baptized and received the Holy Spirit? I implore you to search this out for yourselves. By doing it yourselves it will ignite a hunger to receive Holy Spirit if you do not already have Him. If you do have Him, He will impart a new level of wisdom of Himself to you.

Acts 9:22 says Saul increased in strength the more he went out, and it confused the Jews that someone that once wanted to knock their heads off, now believed as they did and was increasing in that belief. How did Saul surpass them so quickly in their walk in Christ? It is because Jesus said Saul was a chosen vessel of His. Fast forward to today's times, is it safe to say that when we do not allow a chosen vessel of Jesus to operate in their calling, through Holy Spirit, we are negating what God wants to be done in the earth, and in His church? Is it fair to say that this is true, and can we admit it? Remember, it is pride that keeps us low, and outside of the will of God, as believers. Some church leaders may say, "how did this person surpass me so quickly in the things of the Spirit and I have been doing church for decades?" If our emotions are not in check as leaders in ministry, guess what starts brewing against those chosen vessels, with Holy Spirit accelerating them? Jealousy, envy, and possibly strife. I have seen this time and time again and it is time for some leaders to check their hearts, thoughts, and emotions, humbling themselves before God, removing all pride, and seeking God on how He desires for His church to operate in His order.

The Attack

Some church leaders are stuck on those highly gifted (the chosen vessels) for ministry, especially in the five-fold. They assume those highly gifted (the chosen vessel) must be brought up in ministry a certain way. Some say spiritual parenting and or mentoring is the only way one can become a minister of the gospel of Jesus Christ. Now, remember, just over a decade ago, no one was putting such emphasis on spiritual parenting as they are today. With the advent of social media, it has become difficult to lasso in all the new ministries popping up that are taking off and doing well for the kingdom of God.

Now, there is this grand emphasis on spiritual parenting center stage, not to really help you, but it's being talked about to stop the new ministries from surpassing the ones that have been extremely financially successful in the brick-and-mortar house of God.

Social media has interrupted the traditional brick-and-mortar way of doing church. So now you have this new crew of ministries coming from "nowhere", let the brick-and-mortar churches tell it. I can tell you where most of them came from, Arabia or Damascus, and other places as well, but we will talk about those other places later in the chapter. Now, you have the individuals that have been in ministry for a while now that are trying their extreme best to get a handle on these Holy Spirit-filled ministries that did not have to go through them or their choice seminary schools. So now the smear campaign has begun to flow, and all the subliminal sermons from the pulpits, and other social media platforms formed against these new ministries. But why? The old church has no way to control the new parts being added to the machine (the church system) that the Creator Himself desires to add for His purposes, advancing His Kingdom.

The old brick-and-mortar leaders start bashing the social media evangelist, prophets, teachers, and the like, saying, "they don't know where they came from", while Jesus already answered this a few times in scripture. I am paraphrasing here, but once when Jesus' disciple John, let Him know a man was in ministry but hadn't come up through following Jesus as closely as the other disciples had. Yet, what the other man was doing was impactful to the kingdom of God. The man was casting out devils in Jesus' name, and it seemed as if it was working. This man had the authority to cast out devils and had a ministry of deliverance all while separated from the initial fold of the 12 disciples that Jesus chose.

> "And John answered and said, Master, we saw one casting out devils in thy name; and we forbad him, because he followeth not with us. And Jesus said unto him, Forbid him not: for he that is not against us is for us."
> (Luke 9:49-50)

What is this text saying to us? It is saying everything that some in the modern church do not want you to grasp. Once again, God has called some to be mentored and or spiritually parented and it is certainly fine and much needed. But what about those that are like the guy mentioned in Luke 9:49-50? The Bible never mentions his name or who he was. Jesus said, "leave him alone."

Moreover, the text in Luke 9:49-50 is giving us a picture of a ministry that started from sheer will and a desire to work for the kingdom of God. And Jesus, being all-knowing, knew the heart of the man, but His disciple John did not see the man's heart concerning his kingdom assignment. This brief look-in, in scripture, shows us that when one's heart is toward God and called to this type of ministry start-up, He will allow you to minister in this manner. Unfortunately, many have not caught this revelation before they start bashing people that start ministry strictly founded on the name of Jesus, through the leading of the Holy Spirit.

Furthermore, this anonymous man in Luke 9:49-50 had a ministry of deliverance by casting out devils. It is obvious that heaven knew who this man was, and his name obviously being registered in heaven also (Luke 10:20). If you stand him alongside the sons of Sceva, mentioned in the book of Acts 19:13-16 , you will notice that this anonymous man was known by the demons that he was able to cast out. The demons that the sons of Sceva attempted to cast out did not know them and attacked them because the sons of Sceva did not have the authority to cast them out. What did this anonymous man have that the sons of Sceva did not have or lack? The anonymous man in Luke 9 was for Jesus, and being partnered with his faith, produced the power and authority to cast out devils in Jesus' name.

It is unfortunate that some within certain ministry groups believe that in order to be called by God, one must have a spiritual lineage, spiritual DNA, as well as a spiritual inheritance. In portions of scripture, that is true. However, Jesus Christ paints us a different picture with this anonymous man in Luke 9:49-50, whom those in certain ministry groups would call rouge. They failed to understand the dispensation, the covenant, and the reason for Christ on the earth. Jesus went to the cross not just for the Jews but for the world. His doing opened His spiritual lineage, His spiritual DNA, and His spiritual inheritance up to the Gentiles, who had no previous identity in the Spirit. Now, these very Gentiles have the opportunity to become grafted into the branch, a spiritual lineage through being adopted by God:

> "Or is He the God of the Jews only? Is He not also the God of the Gentiles? Yes, of the Gentiles also, since there is one God who will justify the circumcised by faith and the uncircumcised through faith." (Romans 3:29-30)

Meaning, those you once could not recognize in the spirit, should now be well luminated, becoming your brothers and sisters in Christ. Jews as brick-and-mortar tradition, and Gentiles as modern-day social media platforms that are the new ministries now taking advantage of the opportunities given to them, we should also recognize them as brothers and sisters in Christ.

It becomes expedient for you to know that you can jump out for massive soul-winning or start building "A gigantic ministry" immediately after you get converted just as Apostle Paul did. The sovereign authority must be the one to send you out, and the "Sovereign Authority", in this case, is Jesus Christ Himself.

The Birthing of a Disciple

Unfortunately, some Christians have had their own version of "On the Road to Damascus encounter" with Jesus, and have jetted out without any proper guidance or direction from Holy Spirit, negating the whole encounter with Jesus Christ, moving in haste. It is possible to be a Saul converted into an Apostle Paul, but this action takes a completely humbling experience with Jesus, just so the individual doesn't get off track in their call to build and soul win with Christ. Saul had an immaculate resume of the law. But Saul/Apostle Paul was converted into the New Covenant, a spiritual awakening. Jesus Christ could use this Spirit-filled Paul, but not the law-stricken Saul before conversion.

This Saul/Apostle Paul route is not expected of everyone. However, we must be mature as the body of Christ, to grasp that Jesus does have the ability to teach people about His ministry and giftings, that He has bestowed upon certain people, the chosen vessels (Acts 9:15). These people are not grander than those that go the traditional route in ministry. They are just mantled in a different way. A mantle is a supernatural covering that signifies one's power and authority in matters concerning the kingdom of God. These mantled individuals must be met in today's way of doing church with leadership that is spiritually mature enough to know that there is a difference in spiritual maturation. For those that have a higher level of maturation, you cannot stifle them. The stifling is done in ignorance at times and sometimes in the knowledge of the truth. Some leaders hold believers back, to a certain degree, because they believe they are being orderly and traditionally correct.

Can I lend a revelation to those in church leadership? Those whom Jesus Christ has sent the route of Arabia before coming to you to receive the right hand of fellowship, have a clear understanding of Kingdom order and ranking, and they will not do anything out of order with Holy Spirit. I know this may be difficult for a lot of people to believe, but what do you think Paul was receiving in Arabia? I can answer that, Paul was receiving prophetic downloads from Holy Spirit on the order of the Kingdom of God. Paul, knowing and hearing of the disciples of Jesus Christ, knew there was an order. However, Holy Spirit downloaded to Paul the kingdom order of heaven. Thus, allowing Paul to never over-step the apostolic leadership that came before him. So, dear leaders, please understand, when Jesus has mantled His chosen vessels, He has mantled them with kingdom order that can only be imparted by Holy Spirit.

Today, this spiritual maturation process is often skipped and is largely missing in America's church system. There are various forms God has in the process of spiritual growth. You may debate, ignore, or fight it, but the spiritual maturing process is a God-given template for godly efficient, and effective ministry. We can no longer skip over this maturation process. Even so, we must be mindful of how He plans to use the individual once He deems the process of their tutelage complete.

THE CHURCH KILL: WHAT IS KILLING THE CHURCH?

It is unfortunate to note that some people that are already in ministry do not want some believers to move an inch as Christ's ambassador. They are threatened by your intimacy with God and your anointing frustrates them, all while they are afraid that you will overtake them. Thus, the famous statement, "stay in your lane" is adopted by many insecure leaders. Your God-given gifts are a threat to them. Hence, they are ready to go the extra mile to stop you, in some settings, but not all. They are like the old prophet that sank the glory of the young prophet. Their advice can be like a dagger that pierced through the young prophet, killing the strict instructions received from the Lord, thus ultimately killing the young prophet. How did he get there? If you study the text in 1 Kings 13:11-27, you will see how the young prophet was manipulated, lied to, and coerced by someone he trusted.

What sponsored the old prophet to misguide the young prophet remains nebulous. The young prophet was gullible because he lacked spiritual maturity. He heard a word from the Lord and was given clear instructions from the Lord. Yet, because of the trust and reverence for one that went before him in prophecy and/or ranking, his elder, so to speak, the young prophet totally ignored the word of God, which consequently cost him his ministry as well as his life. If given another opportunity, I believe the young prophet wouldn't repeat that same mistake. To know that he never got another chance to fulfill his purpose because of the word of an elder-ranking prophet, which was a lie orchestrated by that elder prophet, is something that we need to be able to discern today. To fulfill your purpose, there is a need to mature rapidly in ministry – both in discernment and anointing, because not everybody will support the vision or mission that God placed in you to carry out. As we see in the text, the older prophet was jealous of the younger one because he had just had a great victory for the kingdom. The naivete of the young prophet had him dining with that which was ready to kill him and the ministry that God placed in the younger prophet.

The Teacher, The Leader, The Appointer

Has the body of Christ truly examined the text of God? Has the church really allowed <u>all</u> five of the fivefold ministries to be in full operation? The answer to both questions is no. The Holy Bible being the body of Christ's text and or study guide, we have allowed men and women to teach it without them really understanding what God's voice or word is saying. Some of these same men and women teaching falsely may not even have Holy Spirit. One thing I know about the word of God is that you must have the Spirit of God to truly be able to preach or teach His gospel error-proof. It is His Spirit that leads you on what to teach and or preach. Jesus Christ, Himself, stated that God had anointed Him to preach the gospel. Teaching the word of Christ is not something that can be taken lightly.

Therefore, Holy Spirit-led teachers in the office are needed because a teacher, led by Holy Spirit, will not allow the error of teaching the text of God incorrectly to stand. They will correct it through the power of the Holy Spirit. The unfortunate thing is most churches won't even allow a teacher to teach the Word of God and the teacher is an office in ministry.

Jesus left the church with five leadership governing offices, to lead His church, and to work with the body of Christ to perfect the saints. The issue with the modern church is that someone made the apostle and prophet the two highest governing giftings, but they are not when concerning the governing and perfecting of the saints. All five are the highest, (i.e. apostle, prophet, teacher, evangelist, pastor). Most do not understand that it is Jesus' design for those that can handle it, for them to operate in all five offices at any given time. Jesus himself did. Some days He was a Pastor, and some days He taught as a Master Teacher (Raboni). Some days, Jesus operated in the gift of evangelism. He prophesied all the time, and He was the Chief Apostle every day. If we pay close attention to Jesus' walk or ministry, He showed us that He even moved in the Spiritual gifts given by Holy Spirit as well.

The Fold

However, this brings me to my next point in scripture, where Jesus informs His disciples of the sheep He has that are not a part of their current fold. So, a question popped into my mind, "who were these sheep, and who was teaching them the things about the kingdom of God?" Jesus went on to say to His disciples, "them He must also bring" and guess what? "They will hear my voice." Hmm, I wonder what Jesus is saying here. Could He possibly be saying that there are people that will be led by His voice and calling for them, just like He did with Apostle Paul in the book of Acts? Or, like the anonymous man we just read about in Luke 9:49-50? That man wasn't a part of the fold, yet he heard the voice of Jesus and He got to work.

On the other hand, Jesus did not stop there. He said, "there shall be one fold, and one Shepherd." (John 10:16). What is proper to summate through Holy Spirit intellect is, that there are some that Jesus will also graft in that may not have the original spiritual lineage or spiritual DNA, but they do now have the spiritual inheritance because of the Cross and Resurrection of Jesus Christ.

Where Do I Go?

I am so glad that question surfaced within you. Once born-again God has a place for a brand-new convert and that is His church. God introduced the church to the world, for it to become a safe haven for those believers that are looking for refuge from the fallen world. A place to cover the believers of God, a place to receive the Word of God, a place to become spiritually healthy, and sober in mind, and a place to receive the love of God. Unfortunately, some churches can be as unhealthy as this world we live in. One of the ways the church is unhealthy is through teaching the wrong doctrine, thus teaching the Bible in error. This can cause aches, pains, bumps, and bruises as a convert tries to grow spiritually in God. The last we all checked, bumps and bruises tend to hurt. For this, the church is in serious need of deliverance.

Church hurt isn't always, "oh girl, they talked about me, they preached on my life from the pulpit," for an example. But the church is growing wrong due to bad doctrine. That is the church hurt I am talking about, the doctrine of devils the Bible speaks of. We have exhausted the gossip church hurt, the sleeping around with members church hurt, the homosexual lifestyle church hurt to name a few, and all those do hurt. The church hurt I am talking about is worse because it negates one's ability to grow past the other church hurts, as I mentioned above. When the doctrine is off or from devils, there will not be any true conviction or repentance. Basically, if the church didn't teach in error, then the power of God would be so strong in our lives as we receive the Word of God, that we would move on from the hurt with healing and deliverance.

The Appointed By God

This brings me to my next point in God's word: If Jesus has sheep of another fold, He may have workers or servants that He may use differently. Examine Matthew 20:1-16, which is a parable that starts out saying, "the kingdom of heaven is like a landowner." In this parable, the landowner is God, He is over all the land, and He now needs some workers to work His field, which equals the church. So, God found Himself some laborers to work His field. They agreed on a monetary amount for a day's work. We'll say the first crew of workers is the brick-and-mortar crew. Then some hours of time passed, let's suppose the hours that the Bible speaks of are years, decades, or even perhaps centuries. So God, the owner of all the land or fields, which once again equals the church, a few hours later (years or decades) sees some people idly standing around in their workplaces or marketplace. This group was actively ready for work and was equipped to work, but were idle.

This second group of workers or servants God saw He saw that they weren't in their proper call in the marketplace. So, He decided to call them to come work and/or serve for Him. These servants agreed to the "whatsoever is right" as far as the amount of pay. Then, God moves down the timeline of history, and He locates another group around the sixth and ninth hour of the day, years, decades, or possibly centuries later. He did the same thing He did with the previous crew of workers/servants. Lastly, the landowner, God, in the eleventh hour sees a group just standing around idle, and God asks, "why stand ye here all the day idle?" These workers were idly standing by, they were ready for hire or to be used by God. Yet, it is worth noting, that in this parable that God Himself is appointing the workers, not man.

Let's give the eleventh-hour worker/servant the title of internet ministry. These are the ones that are going to use the platforms given them to start what Christ called them to do. These eleventh-hour workers in verses seven of Matthew 20 said "we are standing", Holy Spirit just spoke and said, "to be seen standing by Him, is to be seen in a ready to go or a ready to work position." Moreover, God the church owner is looking down the timeline and looking at the need of His people and the need for His church to have great workers in it, but they are standing idle. They are in the ready position but idle! So, the landowner weighing the need verses availability, He goes out and finds His own workers. In addition, the eleventh-hour workers tell the collective of the entire parable and its multi layered meaning.

The first group of workers are the system, the structure, while the next group of workers were workers that were in the marketplace called there but idle in the work of the kingdom. The sixth and ninth align with the first two. As we get to the eleventh hour the Landowner had to ask them why they were idle. Holy Spirit revealed to me, that the first three groups were supposed to be the last group's benchmark on how to work in His kingdom. The ball was dropped. The Landowner is perplexed as He asked them why they are idle. At this point, there has been plenty of examples of how to do the work, why isn't the work being done? The eleventh-hour workers told the Landowner "No MAN has hired us." No one appointed them, no one saw them to open a door for them with the keys to the kingdom of heaven.

God being God and the owner of man, time, and land (the church) had to do the appointing. Man, for some reason would not move without God pushing them into their places. What I learned from this parable is, God sees those that are standing idle, in a ready position, with nowhere to work. I learned that God could do the appointing of whomever He desires, to work for Him. I learned, do not wait on man to open things to you, just stay in a ready position and God will find a use for you. I also learned, in this parable God hadn't appointed spiritual parents or required a spiritual lineage or DNA test to use these servants on His land. He did not say having a spiritual lineage or spiritual DNA was a wrong or right process, but at the time of His need He did not require it to work for Him.

I like how Holy Spirit used the different times of the day to signify the different eras of the church. I like how the church is talked about as a reference to the kingdom of heaven and breaking it down further with the vineyard being that place of the church, as well as the church needing laborers. I enjoyed how the scripture noted that the reward for working in the kingdom of heaven is the same across the span of time. It did not matter if it were the brick-and-mortar crew, the televangelist crew, or the last hour works using the available platforms to get the gospel out around the world.

As I was in prayer this very morning, I kept hearing the Lord say in my spirit to wait on Him, wait on Him. He said it several times, then He said while you are waiting on me, be doing something that I can use once the wait is over (i.e. standing in the marketplace). Looking at the text of Matthew 20:1-16, I get it. The people were idle. But while they were idly waiting, they were standing. Just because they were idle, it did not mean they were not ready. I looked up the word idle and one of the synonyms is inactive. These groups of people in the text were waiting to be activated or actively waiting on God to be moved into their spiritual assignments. Another word for idle is unused, why weren't these workers being used? But, if you look at the word stand, we know that the word stand is an action word, they were doing something. Do not sit and wait on God, stand, and wait on Him. Be in the go position where all it takes is a step from there when the Lord says, "Go."

In this chapter, I wanted to attempt to show the church and the body of Christ, the other side of the coin. On one side of the coin, there is a group of individuals that need the traditional route of being brought up through ministry rankings. On the other side, there is a group Holy Spirit will call forth Himself and that group is to be respected just as well as the ones that went up the ministry ranks. The ones Holy Spirit calls forth may do things slightly different than the traditional church because they're going strictly by His lead. The rest of the church must have someone mature enough to see God is using whom He appointed and not to bash them while they are doing the work of the kingdom. If Jesus says, "leave them alone", why can't the leaders of the church do the same?

CHAPTER 6

YOUR GIFT DOES NOT FIT THE SYSTEM

Are your spiritual gifts fit for the kingdom of God's use or fit for the current church system?

I pray that by now you do know there is a difference in the kingdom of God's model of church versus the current carnal church system model. There are different types of churches in the United States. In today's model of the church, in the predominantly African American church in the United States, these churches can assemble very quietly. They sit there attentively, listening to the teaching or preaching and getting all they need. Holy Spirit doesn't display much of His emotion or fiery personality. I am by no means saying Holy Spirit doesn't show up in these churches, because He does. He is just displaying a calmer side to Himself. I've heard some churches don't even have instruments in them and they actually forbid them from being played in the sanctuary. That is unfortunate because Holy Spirit is a singer, songwriter, and poet, He dances, smiles, and so much more. There have been millions of God-ordained songs over the years, but none of them will be heard there.

Then you have some churches that are more charismatic. Charismatic churches are those that fascinate, captivate, allure, appeal, and are very attractive. These churches are attractive because they appeal to a particular need of the people. Not everyone that goes to these charismatic churches are in need of Jesus Christ, some are there because of the allure that being in the service may bring. Secondly, some are there to bolster what they are in need of, a business connection and/or a marketing deal. A lot of these types of churches draw enormous numbers each week, which is great for them. But are the gathered souls being transformed from worldly to kingdom?

Then there are some churches that are so engulfed in man-made tradition, that anything that looks like the glory of God is shot down, not received and whomever God has given His glory to, will be looked at like an outsider to the man-made traditionalists. Jesus Christ got on the Pharisees about cleaning their bowls and plates on the outside (looking the part), Yet being filthy within (Luke 11:39). Then there are the churches that meet for an hour with power. There are some that have theater-style lighting, seating, gourmet coffee, and big screens. They also have dimmed lights, setting an ambiance of holiness and worship. I say all of this to compare the variation of churches in essence with the variation of our access to spiritual giftings.

If there are various styles of having church, could it be that God has a variation of our spiritual gifts that He chooses to use through His people? Imagine these chosen vessels with the same exact gifting through Holy Spirit's same power. We would all be doing the same type of healing, prophesying, singing, and ministering all while trying to serve people with various needs of deliverance. That wouldn't work. So, God created each of us uniquely to be gifted in the area He chooses, and usually, the gifts are attached to our personality, character, and strengths.

Holy Spirit desires for us that have His Spirit, to operate in what He gives us and apply it in the will of God for kingdom purposes. How do we apply the application of our giftings, aren't we to be taught the application? Who are the teachers of the application, is it all left up to the Teacher Holy Spirit, or has God called out some that are Gifted to teach the application of our Spiritual gifts? If God gives them, He intends for us to use them. Hence, the question does your spiritual gifts fit the current church system?

Does the current church system allow those who are gifted to apply their gifts in the church setting, or are we to sit in the pew loaded with gifts, crowned with blessings, and witty inventions lying dormant? I think not, there is a time coming real soon when those held back are going to break forth in their callings. The false church won't be able to stop it. We just need true teachers to stand up to what has been thumbing them down. There is an enormous amount of gifted capabilities locked inside these individuals, and most are truly unaware of it. I pray this book is the key to unlocking what the enemy has used to shut us out of our true stance in the earth as believers. Our gifts are supposed to profit the body of Christ, not just the chosen few. No more will it just be a few that receive from God while the rest sit and hope one day. No! The keys to the kingdom will be released and we are going to walk through every divinely appointed door.

Here is another question. Does your divine spiritual impartation and the gifts given by God after that impartation, truly make room for you, or are they shunned in certain false and carnal churches? The Holy Bible says that our gifts will make room for us and put us amongst great people.

> "A man's gift maketh room for him, and bringeth him before great men." (Proverbs 18:16)

God prefers to have His children gifted here on the earth and gave us the promise that our gifts would make room for us. If God gives wisdom freely, would He not give us the ability to invent and create things on the earth, like witty inventions, giving us knowledge and the understanding of how to use these things to carry out His will?

> "For wisdom is better than rubies; and all the things that may be desired are not to be compared to it. I wisdom dwell with prudence, and find out knowledge of witty inventions." (Provers 8:11-12)

> "Wisdom is the principal thing; therefore get wisdom: and with all thy getting get understanding." (Proverbs 4:7)

The world is not the only place that has smart people. God's kingdom has geniuses overflowing. So why aren't they on full display or being utilized? Why are so many sitting in church, full of gifts, not being used and not given the room to increase? Why are their witty inventions overlooked or locked up, by the church?

Why when we get a clear understanding from God, is it usually smothered and choked out by churches and/or church leaders? Why isn't our wisdom a principal in the church?

Our gifts making room for us must be obtained via the knowledge of how to utilize these gifts. This is where church leadership is supposed to come into play. For example, Holy Spirit, being a Teacher, and Jesus leaving the church with some teachers, the appointing of Holy Spirit-filled and led teachers is what is needed and must go forth now in the name of Jesus. I believe once people read this book and learn that their gifts making room for them come from being taught, we will start actively pursuing the knowledge Holy Spirit has readily available to us, through His teachers. The gifts of the Holy Spirit are given to cause an abundance of life in an individual as well as the body of Christ. Why are we not all living an abundance of life if our gifts are for increasing? We must now check our learning and understanding.

Understanding what God has for us in this hour is key to the next generation walking into their abundance freely. What we do today will aid that. The catalyst for this all starts by getting an understanding. Living life without an understanding of the basic principle of why we are here is a blinder. The Holy Bible inspires us to seek wisdom because it is the principal thing. Next, we are asked to, in all the things we can possibly accumulate, accumulate understanding. Understanding has vision attached to it. With a clear understanding, we can see exactly where God wants us to go. We can see our purpose for life if the eyes of our understanding are becoming enlightened.

"That the God of our Lord Jesus Christ, the Father of glory, may give unto you the spirit of wisdom and

> revelation in the knowledge of Him: The eyes of your understanding being enlightened; that ye may know what is the hope of his calling, and what the riches of the glory of his inheritance in the saints, And what is the exceeding greatness of his power to us-ward who believe, according to the working of his mighty power."
> (Ephesians 1:17-19)

With the eyes of our understanding enlightened, we can assess the proper application of our gifts. This makes getting an understanding imperative because it puts us as a body in the proper context to assess, equip, and send out. Without understanding we will continue to just have butts in seats, not going out into the world as kingdom ambassadors for Christ. Our gifts are not given by Holy Spirit for us to just sit in the pews every Sunday. They are meant to go out but to profit withal that is in the body of Christ.

By understanding our spiritual makeup, so to speak, we then can grasp the dynamics of our purpose and our giftings. These dynamics are only unlocked in their holiest form through the Holy Spirit by the word of God and by trusting in Holy Spirt led leadership teachings. Because many of us know that the gifts and callings are without repentance, but we should be desiring to become gifted only from a repented heart. Any other gifting is false and not from Holy Spirit.

The Church Cult and The Church Mafia

The impartation of our spiritual gifts can be considered as the initiation of equipping us of our gifts, but consequently, some of us have run into some churches that are more cult-like than Kingdom of God-like. What is a church cult? Who runs it? Church cults are often run by individuals that are complete narcissists. A person who is in love with control and is extremely in love with controlling the people of God. This church leader plays both sides to get what they want. For example, they use mind games, voice hypnosis, and atmosphere or environment manipulation. They are masters at manipulating people and putting people against each other. They are money centered, self-centered, the look-at-me type, that looks holy on the outside. They tend to prop themselves up to be grandeur in the spirit realm. You are low and they are high all the while dangling this carrot in front of you, it's the imaginary wealth carrot that we all seem to want, glamourized by prosperity preachers.

The church cult leaders are excellent at recruiting followers, they say all the things you want to hear, using the Lord's name to keep your attention. They pervert the Bible (the Word of God), and they lie on God, saying He said something, and God never said it. They seek out and recruit the spiritual novice, those that do not understand their gifts and callings yet. Some even go so far as to use black magic spells to get members. The cult leader will tell you there is no other church like his or hers. They say things like, "you won't be taught this anywhere else because God only gave this revelation to me." Dear Saints, of the Most High God, be very careful out there when choosing a church. Make sure Holy Spirit has truly called you to that place. The devil is very crafty at deception, but Jesus is wiser.

Unfortunately, when they have another sect of the church that thinks they are the owners of the church, these are they that run the church of God like a mafia. A church mafia is a network of evil-doers that use God as a front to gain access to affluent means. They are tightly joined together, no newcomers unless you take a vow of secrecy or are born into it. Sounds a lot like frats and sororities. The church mafia will kill you, if not physically, then mentally, emotionally, and verbally by the assassination of your character, and/or spiritually. They will kill your name, attempting to destroy your character and good reputation with others. What they really want is for you not to work in the kingdom through the ministry that God Himself placed inside of you. They are really trying to kill that before you even get started. They start before you even get a true understanding of who you are in Christ. Like Joseph and his brothers, they wanted to kill him off before he could walk into his purpose. Please read through the story of Joseph in Genesis chapters 37-50 to understand how this text parallels why the church mafia wants to kill you before the Lord appoints you in your calling.

Joseph's brothers were jealous of him because their father Israel loved Joseph. Joseph was the son of his old age. I personally believe Israel loved the last two sons differently because those sons were by the wife he so loved the most. Yet, Joseph's brothers could pick up on the deep love Israel had for Joseph. Israel didn't make the envy any better. He then gives Joseph a mantle (coat of many colors) heavy laden with giftings. Each color of Joseph's mantle meant a different gift. One of Joseph's gifts was to dream and interpret dreams. Joseph had a couple of dreams; he was so excited about them, and he tells his brothers. Some in ministry say Joseph was being arrogant in telling his dreams. But I don't believe that at all because I can tell my dreams to my sister or family members, and they may not even know the interpretation and won't get jealous of the dream spoken, like Joseph's brothers.

Moreover, when Joseph told his dreams, what stood out to me was his brothers' gifts. Joseph's brothers were able to interpret the dreams he spoke to them. That is what stuck out the most because, here are the brothers envious of Joseph because of his calling, but they totally overlooked their very own giftings that if you keep reading the Bible you will read that there were many kings that had dreams and needed or demanded an interpreter. Even Joseph's gift of interpretation would be needed by the pharaoh of Egypt. So, what is missing is that even his brothers could have been used by God if their eyes weren't evil. But God used their evil eyes, just as He uses Satan to turn his evil around for our good. God did the same for Joseph, the nation that he was second in command over, and Joseph's entire family in the end.

Joseph went on to do exactly what his mantle had covered him to do. What the enemy did via his brothers was to prolong the process. So, that is a biblical look at some of the characteristics of the church mafia. Some of them are gifted too but because their eye is so evil, they do not realize that their gifts are much needed for the true church and kingdom of God.

Another reason the church mafia wants to stop you, just like Joseph's mantle, the mantle that you carry will always reveal the truth. When Joseph came into the purpose of the dreams that were revealed to himself and his family, with him having a high position and saving his nation and his entire family from starvation and death, it revealed Joseph's brother's jealousy and the detestable lie they told.

The mantle on your life, when you are filled with the Holy Spirit and have a pure heart, automatically shines a holy light in dark areas on the lie or lies being spoken and/or carried out by the false church and church mafia's leadership. Therefore, an attempt to put a bowl over your lamp (holy light) is automatic, so the truth will not go forth, to keep the lie from being exposed, and stunt the growth of the true church. This makes church hurt easy and takes your focus if you allow it. This is the design and purpose of the enemy to keep you from going forth in your purpose and calling. "The Church Needs Deliverance" from the false church and the church mafia!

CHAPTER 7

WHAT'S WRONG WITH MY PRAISE AND WORSHIP?

If you genuinely and intensely praise God, and the glory of God manifests in the service, you will be watched as if you are breaking their church protocol or laid down rules concerning praise and worship. Why? There is a supernatural move of God in that environment. If we serve the same God and have the same Holy Spirit, a move of God in service should prompt you to allow Holy Spirit to take over and do what He enters the service to do. Because you understand the movement of God, and how He wants His church to function, they will try to make you seem unfit for that church. They will make you feel unwelcome and rejected; consequently, you will gladly go where the Holy Spirit is freely moving, and brethren are loving.

Perhaps you're wondering if we are collectively in the same place praising the same Lord, how is it they quickly notice your praise and worship? The answer is simple. Although you're yet to understand whom Christ has called you to be, they can spot you because of your radiant light. Like Satan, most of these fake church leaders can appear as angels of light. So, it becomes easy for the devil to perceive the real light of God beaming all over you. I am giving you a glimpse of what it is like to see in the Spirit. Something that isn't taught at a high level in most modern churches.

> "For such are false apostles, deceitful workers, transforming themselves into the apostles of Christ. And no marvel; for Satan himself is transformed into an angel of light." (2 Cor. 11:13-14).

In some churches, there is a real push to stifle the Holy Spirit. You say how is this? The way Holy Spirit is stifled in the church is by placing a stopwatch on His service. I have seen with my own two eyes; Holy Spirit is ready to usher in deliverance in service and as soon as He gets ready to move on our behalf, delivering and setting people free from chains of bondage and wickedness, because of the restricting of time in that moment, they shut out and stifle Holy Spirit, quenching the Holy Spirit in that moment. The false church knows what it is doing at that very moment and Holy Spirit does also.

Unfortunately, due to ignorance, believers aid in this because we don't see the spirit behind these things, so we're good with an hour of service. Many times, we are so ready to get home to see our favorite teams play, cook our Sunday dinners, and get prepared for the work week, not knowing that we may be missing out on healings, deliverance, and many other things that Holy Spirit wants to impart during church service, but we limit or quench Him because of our time. In ignorance, we don't know that this is an enemy tactic. What have we missed from God, being in a rush? Also, we must choose the place where we worship God wisely, where His Holy Spirit is able to move without inhibition.

Deliverance takes time and actual work. I've seen some ministries shut down healing and anointing because working the altar is just that, a job in the spirit. And I have seen ministers get down and dirty casting demons out. So, what causes Holy Spirit to enter a church service? Holy Spirit enters a service because of the scripture that states, "For where two or three gathered together in my name, there am I in the midst of them." (Matthew 18:20). Unfortunately, Holy Spirit is easily quenched by us humans. One thing we have mastered as a body of believers is quenching or grieving the person, Holy Spirit. Yet, in an assembly, He is searching for two or three just to be able to enter the room.

Praising and worshiping Jesus Christ is another way Holy Spirit shows up. The first way was by gathering in the name of Jesus. Yet, being in service myself, as I looked over the congregation briefly because I'm praising the Lord, I noticed that everyone is having their own worship experience. I have been in some places where when there is genuine and intense praise and worship going on, it is shunned and not wanted. Have you ever heard someone say, "it don't take all that!"? My answer to that is, "for some it does!" It baffled me to see such a lack of understanding of the expression of holiness in an assembly of people. There is a spiritual gauge that measures the magnitude of our praise and worship, it measures our capacity to yield to holiness. This gauge of the spirit determines the measurement of glory in the room. Some of us think we are just meeting for other butts-in-seats experience but just remember, it only takes two or three that show up with the right spirit before the Lord, for the measurement to begin.

We have examples of the temple or cities being measured by angles in linen, so they show up today also.

> "And there was given me a reed like unto a rod: and the angel stood, saying, Rise, and measure the temple of God, and the altar, and them that worship therein."
> (Revelations 11:1)

In certain church services, you can feel Glory ready to burst at the seams, only if it was truly welcomed. There is a supernatural move of God in the environment anyone spiritually attuned with the Spirit of holiness (Rom 1:4) can grasp, and can understand what God wants, but you can't do anything because you don't lead that congregation. The only thing one can do is intercede. I've seen it, the unchurched get aligned with Holy Spirit in these congregations, and Holy Spirit causes them to cut up, not fleshy, but holy. Consequently, I have seen some make that unchurched person seem unfit to praise the Lord, or I have heard them say the person that is praising is seeking attention.

In this brief observation (because I'm trying to receive from God in the service, but God gets my attention to see a matter for this writing moment), I wondered, isn't this the house of the Lord? Leave these, praising the Lord in truth alone, and let them praise the Lord in holy order of course. Stop making praise and worship a rejected moment.

We have biblical evidence of what it looks like to praise and worship God in the order of spirit and truth. King David, a man after God's own heart and an apple of God's eye, King David, not perfect as a man nor a king, but he had something! What was it that David had? King David had humility, love for God's presence, and a willingness to correct himself right where he errored at. King David also had God's attention because David was the only one willing to knock the head off a giant that tormented His people.

The army of the children of Israel feared Goliath. Goliath was a blasphemer against the Living God and David was not hearing that. David also had evidence of the strength and power of God. While in David's preparation season, David dismantled the strength and power of a lion and a bear with his bare hands.

In addition, king David had a real relationship with the Living God. This relationship consisted of worshiping and praising so much so, that David's praise may have seemed radical to some, but had a purpose in God. God's Spirit was in David's presence so much that David begged God not to ever take His presence away from him. The reason we are to never stifle the Holy Spirit is because His presence will leave us. And as a body, we cannot afford to have the presence of God leave us.

An example of David's radical praise, which was pleasing to God, was when David went and brought the Ark of God (The Ark of the Covenant) from Obed-Edom to the City of David with gladness. Obed-Edom was overly blessed because the Presence of God Himself was with them, as the Ark was the Presence of God. David knew that having the Presence of God with him was going to bless his house and all the house of Israel. As the Ark of God was being carried to the City of David, after 6 paces, David sacrificed oxen and fatted sheep unto the Lord. Then, David danced before the Presence of God, honoring Him, he danced so hard that he danced out of a layer of his clothing.

> "Wearing a linen ephod, David was dancing before the LORD with all his might, while he and all Israel were bringing up the ark of the LORD with shouts and the sound of trumpets. As the ark of the LORD was entering the City of David, Michal daughter of Saul watched from a window. And when she saw King David leaping and dancing before the LORD, she despised him in her heart."
> (2 Samuel 6:14-16)

> "Then David returned to bless his household. And Michal the daughter of Saul came out to meet David, and said, How glorious was the king of Israel to day, who uncovered himself to day in the eyes of the handmaids of his servants, as one of the vain fellows shamelessly uncovereth himself! And David said unto Michal, It was before the LORD, which chose me before thy father, and before all his house, to appoint me ruler over the people of the LORD, over Israel: therefore, will I play (music and dance) before the LORD." (2 Samuel 6:20-21)

David's wife Michal was embarrassed by David moving in glory, honoring, and praising in the Presence of God and she egregiously mocked David. What she did not know was that she was mocking God also, simply by mocking David. She only saw an outward display, thinking that David was attempting to be seen by the handmaids of his servants for attention, seeing with her emotions. So my question was, as I got an understanding of the scripture, what was blocking David's wife from receiving the Spirit of the Lord and joining David and the house of Israel in honoring before the Presence of God? David didn't care who was around or how they perceived him, he sought the opportunity to praise and honor the Lord. A wife not willing to align with her husband's praise and worship is instantly disobedient to our Lord and out of order.

David's wife, in today's church, would be one that would say, "It don't take all that." What David's wife Michal was doing was seeing with her emotions and was jealous, not knowing or considering that her house and her entire lineage would be blessed by the Presence of God entering the City of David. She could not see past what she perceived in her own eyes and in her own heart. Because she mocked David, thus ultimately mocking God, she bore no children that would partake in the blessings that David and the house of Israel would receive until the day she died.

Do not mock the praise of a believer that you may deem radical or overly excessive, thinking that the believer is seeking attention. You could be mocking God and thus blocking or shutting down God's original plan to bless you and your entire lineage. Instead, praise and honor in the Presence of God in a way that will get His attention and don't worry about how others perceive you, just as David did.

Similar to what we witness in some congregations, many ministers of the gospel of Jesus Christ can attest to this. Service can be high in the Spirit, many are up praising and worshipping the Lord and you will have those that just stand or sit around as to just spectate, watching others, with their arms folded and a straight face. Some will even mock others right there in the service. What do you do when the mocking comes from those that are supposed to be the ministers or leaders?

Eyes of Our Understanding

On this note, the saints of God should put on their spiritual lenses to perceive the devil at work. But unfortunately, a lot of us have not been taught the things of the Spirit. Trust me, many in church leadership conceal spiritual realities, and it is deliberate and by design. But as I settled to write this, I heard the Holy Spirit declaring that things are changing, and this change will be rapid. Our spiritual lenses play an important part in how we discern things of the Spirit. Discernment is one of the spiritual gifts given by Holy Spirit, that can be activated by impartation. Discernment helps us in our spiritual vision. Therefore, in scripture, the Lord would ask people in the Holy Bible, "what do you see?" How we see is extremely important to how we lead in ministry.

Fit for Kingdom or Fit for Church

Now, two alternatives are available before us – fit for the kingdom of God or fit for the church. It is necessary to make God's ordained choice. Becoming fit for the kingdom is the divine (heavenly) realm while being fit for church only is the human (carnal) realm. The kingdom realm breeds a spiritual atmosphere, while the human realm culminates in a sensual atmosphere. In a carnally dominated atmosphere, the things of God's kingdom will neither be received nor valued. An emotional (unspiritual) church completely detests the kingdom of God. This type of church barely desires the wholeness of God's kingdom. Such churches may claim a form of godliness but will deny the manifestation of God's power in the long run.

"This know also, that in the last days perilous times shall come. For men shall be lovers of their own selves, covetous, boasters, proud, blasphemers, disobedient to parents, unthankful, unholy, Without natural affection, trucebreakers, false accusers, incontinent, fierce, despisers of those that are good, Traitors, heady, highminded, lovers of pleasures more than lovers of

God; Having a form of godliness, but denying the power thereof: from such turn away." (2 Timothy 3:1-5)

A lukewarm church can showcase the performance and semblances of a firebrand church. Still, it is not the true tabernacle of God. It is harrowing that the human eyes cannot see the rottenness cover-up by religion and man-made traditions in the lukewarm church.

A Burdened Heart for the Breaking System

"Brethren, my heart's desire and prayer to God for Israel is, that they might be saved. For I bear them record that they have a zeal of God, but not according to knowledge. For they, being ignorant of God's righteousness, and going about to establish their own righteousness, have not submitted themselves unto the righteousness of God. For Christ is the end of the law for righteousness to every one that believeth." (Romans 10:1-4)

Often, I ruminate and rue over the church's system and standard that's rapidly collapsing in America. I see an urgent need to mend and reverse this situation. It is like a burden, a fire truly shot up through my bones. My strongest desire has always been the health of God's House of prayer and the people that go to it. Meanwhile, I realized that ignorance is the first cause of the increasing disintegration of God's house or flock. I'm aware that some of the leaders involved are naïve; they don't know the supernatural implications of what they are doing, being encapsulated by the tradition repeatedly taught for years. Whatever the Holy Spirit whispers will just be disregarded by some of them. Thus, grieving Him because of the quenching of the fire He wants to use to engulf the church or people of God. Holy Spirit has a goal to keep us from becoming a lukewarm people.

The most painful thing is that this misconception has aborted the genuine call of a lot of God's children. It has restrained the church in no small way. This spiritual darkness has hindered the true movement of God from breaking forth in our midst. The good news is that the Holy Spirit revealed that this barrier will soon roll away, as established in the bible.

"And all thy children shall be taught of the Lord; and great shall be the peace of thy children." (Isaiah 54:13).

Another pain point or burden is illiteracy. False teaching is a silent destroyer, especially in the church of God. When a heretic seed of doctrine is planted in people's hearts, many years of right teachings may not be able to uproot it completely. The heart of a spiritual infant is like fertile soil. Whatever is sown into it will grow fast and grow deeper like tap roots. Hence, the early apostles didn't joke with their doctrine. False doctrine is a sure cause of one becoming unfit for kingdom because what is being taught is disqualifying that person's true supernatural awakening in Christ.

"Take heed unto thyself, and unto the doctrine; continue in them: for in doing this thou shalt both save thyself, and them that hear thee." (1 Timothy 4:16).

The third cause of disintegration is that the true five-fold ministry teachers have not been given the stage or space that Holy Spirit desires for them to have. So, when the Spirit-led teachers are silenced, it hinders the people of God from getting the structured teaching needed from the Holy Spirit. Then, we begin to embrace carnal teachings and fables of men that becomes inevitable. We began to settle for the one-line scripture and two-hour motivational-speaker sermons. The Bible calls this a whitewashing of the word. The philosophies of men.

This kind of sermon doesn't offer bread to the starving soul or succor to the battered. In most cases, it will lead to dramatic physical activities and/or a works-only ministry. This type of church experience can quench the Holy Spirit and merely attract more people. No doubt, some of us will absorb it. First, we are carnal-minded, and it feeds our flesh; hence, we will go with it. Second, because the Holy Spirit is not present in our lives fully. We fail to understand how important the teaching gift of Jesus Christ is to the body of Christ. Fortunately, the Holy Spirit is about to erase this denying ordained teachers their kingdom role and space.

CHAPTER 8

THE VIOLENT TAKE IT BY FORCE

Something that is hard to digest, is that there are demonic gatekeepers monitoring the pulpits and pews at this very hour. Unfortunately, the enemy of God's people has crept into the church. To be honest, as we recall in the history of the first-century church or even Jesus' ministry, we see Satan has never really left the church. He has continued to pierce his eyes into the things of the kingdom of God. Satan has successfully manipulated some of the very elect of God because the devil knows how to deceptively maneuver and get to our weak points as humans. All he needs to do is to feed our flesh and starve our spirit. This is the war between flesh and spirit:

> "For the flesh lusteth against the Spirit, and the Spirit against the flesh: and these are contrary the one to the other: so that ye cannot do the things that ye would."
> (Galatians 5:17)

Satan, our archenemy, has the advantage of being ancient and at one point he stood in the presence of the Most High God. While most of us, not to our recollection or remembrance, have had the divine inference that puts us in the presence of God's wisdom from the beginning, gaining kingdom wisdom before birth to help us navigate this world, hurdling over the enemy's tactics and deceptive schemes.

Satan has stored information about you, your family, and the traits of your lineage. He started at the beginning of man with Adam and Eve. Can you imagine the data that Satan has stored about your family line? He is a master con; he is an ancient creature with the memory of patterns as well as cycles that have taken place over time throughout humanity. There is nothing new under the sun (Ecclesiastes 1:9). He is not omniscient or omnipresent, he just studies and frequently targets us for attack, and he has done this since the creation of man. He has help in this area of doing his dirty work in this fallen world. He is in the business of recruiting people that will align with him against the body of Christ.

It is unbecoming, I must admit, that some of these aligning partners have crept into the pulpit, occupying leadership positions within the church. Therefore, it must always come to mind that judgment will start from the Lord's house because of this reason. God desires order in the house of the Lord always. And when we have allowed Satan to infiltrate the church, God will turn the table over. It is not hidden that many professing Christians have lost their lives (eternally) to hell by adopting certain man-made traditions and fabricated lies, supporting, and teaching the doctrine of devils.

Dear ministers of the gospel, try to align yourself with the Holy Spirit's pattern of leading the church and stop being used by Satan. We must endeavor to be usable vessels of honor, fit for the Lord's vineyard only. The truth must be accurately taught because the kingdom's demands are totally different from worldly demands. The Bible commands that you should seek the kingdom of God first and His righteousness, and all these things will be added to you (Matt. 6:33).

God is not adding anything that He has not empowered you to do. Let's start there first. Instead, God wants you to become born again, develop a genuine relationship with Him, and maintain a burning desire for the Father's will, with the Holy Spirit guiding you and teaching you the true design and will for God's church. What will you gain in return for serving Him? You will gain everything you need to become blessed on earth. As well, you gain eternity in glory preferably. You will not lack a thing when you seek the kingdom first. When we are seeking the kingdom, we are actually seeking God. "For thine is the kingdom and the power and the glory, forever and ever" the bible states.

At this point, I know my message is probably getting a lot of misinterpretations attached to it. It is not unusual to resist the truth. However, there is nothing you can do against the truth but be for the truth.

> "For we can do nothing against the truth, but for the truth." (2 Cor. 13:8).

Expectedly, the false-church systems will struggle to protect their franchise, but their ungodly system will inevitably collapse. But it won't collapse without fighting the truth. The frankness of this book may also be another plausible reason that church leadership may think I am launching a personal attack or coming for them (I am not). The Spirit of God only led me to deliver His message and beam His light on a pseudo-church system that is laissez-faire about the advancement of God's kingdom or the growth of His people.

Why does the Kingdom of Heaven Suffer Violence?

Oftentimes, we talk about how the kingdom of heaven suffers violence (Matthew 11:12), but many don't really understand the crux of this scripture. What violence does the kingdom of heaven suffer? Why does the kingdom of heaven have to suffer violence in the first place? This portion of the bible has been loosely quoted and wrongly interpreted many times, and I understand why there's a misinterpretation. Contrary to what many believers have now come to associate it with, this scripture refers to the wicked. It's about exposing what wickedness does to prevent the people of God and how the enemy robs believers of the glory of God's kingdom.

> "And from the days of John the Baptist until now the kingdom of heaven suffereth violence, and the violent take it by force. For all the prophets and the law prophesied until John." (Matthew 11:12-13)

Let us further examine this scripture with a historical and revelatory lens, through the Holy Spirit. From the days of John the Baptist until now, this very day, the kingdom of heaven suffers violence, and the violent take it by force. Before John the Baptist, it was the prophets and the law that prophesied. Why was it from the days of John the Baptist that the kingdom of heaven suffers violence?

> "Behold, I send My messenger, And he will prepare the way before Me, And the Lord, whom you seek, Will suddenly come to His temple, Even the Messenger of the covenant, In whom you delight. Behold, He is coming." Says the Lord of hosts." (Malachi 3:1)

John the Baptist was the first witness to bear witness of the Light, the true Light that gives light to every man coming into the world, that those who believe would receive the right to become children of God and have access to the kingdom, such as before the fall of man, through the shed blood of Jesus, the Christ, the New Covenant. Before John, it was the law and the prophets, from John until now is the kingdom.

> "In those days came John the Baptist, preaching in the wilderness of Judaea, And saying, Repent ye: for the kingdom of heaven is at hand. For this is he that was spoken of by the prophet Esaias, saying, The voice of one crying in the wilderness, Prepare ye the way of the Lord, make his paths straight." (Matthew 3:1-3)

It is the desire of the enemy to strip those who truly believe, from their access and knowledge of their access to the kingdom because the enemy's access is denied for all eternity. The enemy was the author of the fall of man and desires for his kingdom to prevail over God's kingdom. The New Covenant reconciled us back to God through the shed blood of Jesus Christ, thus annihilating the power of darkness over those that now believe that God sent His only begotten Son to die for our sins, that if we believe in Him, we will not perish, but have everlasting life (John 3:16). This is why the kingdom of God suffers violence. The enemy attempts to fight us tooth and nail to keep us from what the blood of Jesus gave us an all-access pass to, the kingdom of God.

How does the enemy seize the kingdom?

The answer is, by violence – in every form. The enemy infiltrates the body of Christ and masquerades as an angel of light, so he is not easily detected. Meanwhile, the enemy is snatching what belongs to us. The violence in the church is orchestrated by these deceitful men and women who have blended themselves with the body of Christ and are now parading themselves as children of God and ministers of righteousness, in leadership roles. These folks serve in different capacities in the church as members, workers, board members, and even preachers. Therefore, the devil tries so hard to excommunicate the true fivefold ministry gifts. Jesus left those gifts to the church, to edify and perfect the whole body, and what better way to edify the body, by teaching the body the things of the kingdom of heaven.

> "And he gave some, apostles; and some, prophets; and some, evangelists; and some, pastors and teachers; For the perfecting of the saints, for the work of the ministry, for the edifying of the body of Christ" (Ephesians 4:11-12)

In addition, the kingdom of heaven includes God's church, they are connected by His Spirit. Jesus tells us in scripture, there has been a violent attack on the kingdom of heaven (church realm). And again, He said this before the church was in existence. The book of Jude informs us that some have crept in unawares. These are those who have attacked the kingdom church of God violently and have perverted the Gospel of Jesus Christ.

> "For there are certain men crept in unawares, who were before of old ordained to this condemnation, ungodly men, turning the grace of our God into lasciviousness, and denying the only Lord God, and our Lord Jesus Christ." (Jude 4)

Moreover, Satan and his cohorts are the violent camp that comes to seize all that belongs to the church and the people of God. They desire to lay hold of our stuff, and to date, have done an excellent job of taking our possessions. God's word says, no good thing will He withhold from you. It also says, to possess your possessions:

> "For the LORD God is a sun and shield: the LORD will give grace and glory: no good thing will He withhold from them that walk uprightly." (Psalm 84:11)

> "But on Mount Zion there shall be deliverance, And there shall be holiness; The house of Jacob shall possess their possessions." (Obediah 1:17)

> "And ye shall dispossess the inhabitants of the land, and dwell therein: for I have given you the land to possess it." (Numbers 33:53)

God has given you everything you need to possess your possessions, your land, the kingdom, which is rightfully ours, being joint heirs with Christ (Romans 8:16-17). The kingdom of heaven from the days of John the Baptist until now is suffering violent acts against it Matthew 11:12 states. John the Baptist had his head severed from his body, which was a violent attack on the kingdom of heaven. Sometime later, Jesus gets mocked, beaten, and nailed to a cross. The cross as much as it has meant victory in the life of the sinner that would be saved by it, in the realm of heaven, the shed blood of Jesus Christ was still a violent act against it. Even before that, another example is Satan entering

Judas to manipulate him to plot against Jesus. This was a violent attack against heaven as well. Stephen in the Book of Acts, is stoned to death for reciting the truth, another violent attack on the kingdom of heaven. Later, the way the apostles were violently murdered or died were violent acts against the kingdom of heaven. I am sure you are grasping the point by now.

So, when did the body of Christ receive the commission to be violent? This scripture has been misinterpreted and I understand why Jesus said it and we take Jesus' words as mostly motivating and encouraging. The truth is this particular scripture is exposing what wickedness does to pervert the people of God. The violence the kingdom suffers is the infiltration of the enemy into the Church of God. The enemy causes inner turmoil and fights members of Christ's body (the church).

Let me explain this revelation that Jesus gave in Matthew 11:12. What Jesus was saying to the disciples was a mystery of heaven. If you read 1 Timothy 1:18, you will read Paul urging Timothy to war a good warfare. Paul is not telling Timothy to violently attack the kingdom of heaven. Why would we violently attack our future spiritual abode? The weapons of our warfare are not carnal, but they are mighty through God for the pulling down of strongholds (2 Corinthians 10:4-5). What demonic stronghold is in the kingdom of heaven? Our warfare is against the kingdom of darkness, not heaven's kingdom.

One may ask, what do violent acts on the kingdom of heaven look like in today's modern church settings? Well, here are a few acts or attacks: molestation in the church, homosexuality in the church, false prophecy for gain, compromising and using the world's gay agenda in the church for gain, using the church in politics, urging the church to vote for candidates that are not endorsed by God, but their policies are based purely on things that are an abomination to God and go against His word, all for gain. Massive, well-constructed, and beautifully adorned buildings, while the adjacent communities are in shambles, with no real outreach for said communities. Here are the classics that are considered violent attacks: calling people witches or jezebels that are really anointed and carry the true gospel of Jesus Christ, gossiping, murdering with the tongue, trying to shut people's ministry down because they don't want to align with you and your false doctrine, this is an additional example of the church mafia if you were still looking for one. Don't judge the messenger, I am hearing Holy Spirit on this, Who is airing His grievances. If we are honest, we know God is not pleased and He really is running thin on the dispensation of grace, that we all have abused and taken for granted.

Today's violence against the kingdom of heaven is literally in the church being taken out on the people of God each Sunday morning. What is it? It is a violent act when the people of God are not being taught the ways of the kingdom. Where the Spirit of the Lord is there is liberty (2 Corinthians 3:17). That is not being taught, how the Spirit of God operates and functions in a fallen world. The church is on such a low level of kingdom it really will take a supernatural move of God to bring us up. But saints, this is a deliberate and violent attack against us. You may not have heard this text put into context in such a manner, but I pray you are catching the revelation. It has been a plot of Satan all along to keep the church in a low realm of the supernatural, so he can continue to make his realm look all the more powerful and appealing to the natural eye. We serve a Jesus that when He said, "I Am He," those that came to arrest Him in the garden of Gethsemane fell completely back off their feet and were laid out.

> "As soon then as he had said unto them, I am he, they went backward, and fell to the ground." (John 18:6)

We, being commissioned to do the greater works are missing out on the true power of Christ Jesus. Many people turn to the kingdom of darkness because they see results. Because they are receiving tutelage in their dark arts to operate in a power that comes from Satan. Meanwhile, Satan's cohorts are in the church thumbing down the kingdom of heaven, violently stripping it from its power. The kingdom of heaven is so gracefully waiting on us to stand up to the attacks. But we have no idea they exist because we have received the wrong teaching. We are currently being taught self-help sermons, how to deal with the narcissist on the job, along with being focused on obtaining riches, cars, and homes. But little do we know, if we were taught the things of the kingdom, we would not have to receive weekly encouraging messages because the power that we would have wouldn't even allow those issues to be prominent. That is another example of a violent attack on the kingdom of heaven (church realm).

In addition, when we get in church and quote Matthew 11:12, the church goes wild, thinking they are violently taking the kingdom of heaven. When that isn't even God's character toward us. Why would He want a violent character in us toward His heavenly realm? I have been in those services where we get excited and begin to shout with joy when this verse is quoted to us. We, in ignorance, are perishing because we are siding with the demonic, not having a true understanding of what this means. I can tell you the angels of heaven will not fight their own abode. When we ignorantly believe we are the ones to commit violent acts against heaven, the angels of the Lord are looking around like I am not tearing anything up in my abode.

But for sheer lack of revelation of scripture, those angelic hosts are fighting demonic hosts that try and kill, steal, and destroy in the heavenly realm. Stealing our stuff, killing our lives, and destroying our destinies all in the realm of heaven before it even hits the earth. Oh God, how we desire for Your will to be done on earth as it is in heaven. Our job as saints is to bombard the kingdom of darkness in prayer to go against the violence going on in the kingdom of darkness.

Demonic Systems

What are some of the systems that Satan uses to violently take the kingdom of heaven (church realm) by force? Satan is using governmental groups, freemasons, eastern stars, fraternities, sororities, the occult, sorcery, black magic, spells, and whatever else they are using to form strongholds and strong delusions in the minds of the people of God. I know this is a little deep and may not be received completely, simply because I just mentioned a lot of people's favorite organizations that they have pledged (tied their souls) to. I can assure you these organizations are not of the Holy Spirit. If the statement about the groups you have pledged to makes you feel angry or attacked, ask the Lord to show you the spirit behind these groups. Many people are unaware that these groups have become their god. It is encouraged that you seek God for the truth about these organizations, renounce it, and ask God for deliverance and He will set you free.

These said organizations and groups are anti-Christ and anti-kingdom of God, even when they say that God is their foundation. False! It's like slapping a Jesus bumper sticker on something that is totally demonic in the sight of the Lord, and truthfully, these groups actively work against God to keep His people from experiencing His powerful Spirit fully, attempting to mix the demonic with holiness. Darkness and light cannot exist together. It is like oil and water; these things do not mix.

> "You shall not sow your vineyard with different kinds of seed, lest the yield of the seed which you have sown and the fruit of your vineyard be defiled." (Deuteronomy 22:9)

> "Be ye not unequally yoked together with unbelievers: for what fellowship hath righteousness with unrighteousness? and what communion hath light with darkness? And what concord hath Christ with Belial? or what part hath he that believeth with an infidel? And what agreement hath the temple of God with idols? for ye are the temple of the living God; as God hath said, I will dwell in them, and walk in them; and I will be their God, and they shall be my people. Wherefore come out from among them, and be ye separate, saith the Lord, and touch not the unclean thing; and I will receive you. And will be a Father unto you, and ye shall be my sons and daughters, saith the Lord Almighty." (2 Corinthians 6:14-18)

A number of these said organizations and groups perform rituals and spells, praying to foreign gods and idols to advocate their agendas. Guess what is at the root of all of this? Yes, it's money, after just pure hate for God and His ways as well as His people. Next is the love of or for money, which takes over a person's mind, body, and spirit. Money becomes their idol/god, and they will do anything to get it. Some of this delusion is done in ignorance but it is still a fact.

A little leaven leavens the whole lump, please be aware of that (Galatians 5:9). Spreading false doctrine is another demonic tactic or system to keep believers separated from the kingdom. Just a little twisting of the word of God and over time, with repetition, there is a whole lot of twisted perversion and mixture, mixed into the word, causing deception and the itching ear syndrome, where we just want to hear a feel-good message but will deny and hate the truth when it is spoken. The violent (Satan and the demons that do his bidding) have taken the truth and many things that belong to us as believers, by force, deceiving many and keeping us from the fullness and wholeness of the kingdom. Thus, "The Church Needs Deliverance."

> "For the time will come when they will not endure sound doctrine, but according to their own desires, because they have itching ears, they will heap up for themselves teachers; and they will turn their ears away from the truth, and be turned aside to fables." (2 Timothy 4:3-4)

> "The Spirit clearly says that in later times some will abandon the faith and follow deceiving spirits and things taught by demons. [2] Such teachings come through hypocritical liars, whose consciences have been seared as with a hot iron." (1 Timothy 4:1-2)

CHAPTER 9

KEEPERS OF KNOWLEDGE AND THE KEYS: THEY WON'T LET YOU ENTER

"Woe unto you, lawyers! for ye have taken away the key of knowledge: ye entered not in yourselves, and them that were entering in ye hindered." (Luke 11:52)

"Woe to you, scribes and Pharisees, you hypocrites! You shut the kingdom of heaven in men's faces. You yourselves do not enter, nor will you let in those who wish to enter." (Matthew 23:13)

Here are two scriptures that give the reader a look at a certain type of leadership. In the modern-day church, these are leaders that know what it takes for you to be blessed but will not offer you any advice. A couple of years ago, I heard two ministry leaders on different occasions say, "they had a word from the Lord for someone but because of that person's "attitude", they would not release the word to that person." Both ministry leaders also have a large following. Before I go any further, these two ministers did not say at any point that the Lord told them not to release the word the Lord gave them for these people because of the person's attitude. Moreover, what these two ministers said brought me to the text in the book of Acts, chapter 9 verses 10 through 19. Which talks about the brief encounter that Ananias and Saul had. Both Saul and Ananias had encounters with the Lord about each other. For Ananias, the Lord came in a vision, called Ananias' name. Ananias responded, "here I am Lord." The Lord proceeds to give Ananias instructions to go meet Saul of Tarsus because Saul had been praying. And in a vision, Saul had seen a man named Ananias coming to lay hands on him, so Saul may regain his sight.

Ananias began to question the Lord about the man Saul. Saul of Tarsus had a bad reputation for doing harm to those who believe in Jesus Christ. So much so, Jesus asked Saul, "why are you persecuting Me?" Jesus Himself. I believe it is safe to say, Saul had a bad attitude toward Jesus and His people. Ananias, skeptical, says to the Lord, "I have heard from many about this man, how much harm he has done to Your saints in Jerusalem."

" And the Lord said unto him, Arise, and go into the street which is called Straight, and enquire in the house of Judas for one called Saul, of Tarsus: for, behold, he prayeth, And hath seen in a vision a man named Ananias

> coming in, and putting his hand on him, that he might receive his sight. Then Ananias answered, Lord, I have heard by many of this man, how much evil he hath done to thy saints at Jerusalem: And here he hath authority from the chief priests to bind all that call on thy name."
> (Acts 9:11-14)

Now that's a bad attitude! Saul had the authority from the chief priest to bind all who called on the name of Jesus. Verse 15 of Acts nine, says the Lord gave Ananias "a word" that word was, "Go, for he (Saul) is a chosen vessel of Mine, to bear My name before Gentiles, kings, and the children of Israel." What!? Both men got "a word" from the Lord about the other. Yet, verse 17 of Acts nine says Ananias went and did exactly what God instructed him to do.

However, Ananias, knowing how bad of a character Saul was, but not really knowing about Saul's recent encounter with God. Saul's reputation and/or attitude did not stop Ananias from obeying the Lord. Remember the text stated that both men had encounters with the Lord. They both received intel on the other's role in their meet-up. The Lord left no one in the dark. Back to the two ministers that withheld the word of the Lord or prophecy from an individual that both said had a "bad attitude". What if Ananias did that same thing to Saul because of Saul's bad reputation? The two ministers must have thought they were the only ones receiving intel from God.

The person's life they were supposed to speak into had an encounter with God also. God told them, "to get to that conference, get to the church, or get to the meeting. The minister has a word for you, they are going to lay hands on you and what you are going through will be lifted." The person obeys the Lord and gets there in the minister's presence and no word. The ministers saw who the word was for, they saw it was you, the chosen vessel, to bear witness before nations, kings, and even your brethren that would give their lives over to Christ.

Quite possibly, your ministry, through Jesus Christ, would be larger than theirs. So now, you do have an attitude, because God is not a man that He should lie. So, somebody is lying, and they are lying on God. Let's say the person did have a bad reputation, what you are doing, in this instance, is having a form of godliness but denying God's power altogether? So, we are saying "the word from the Lord" had no power to destroy the attitude? No, these are those that have the keys of knowledge but won't give them to you. These are those that shut the kingdom of heaven in a man's face and still won't let you go in. But God always has a ram in the bush. He will get the word to you and these spiritual hoarders will go on doing what they do. Ananias' willingness to obey God's word ranked higher in the kingdom of God than Saul's earthly ministry, which caused Ananias to surpass Saul as a disciple of Christ, only through Ananias' obedience. Saul went on to be a master builder of the Lord's church.

Saul went on spreading the gospel of Jesus Christ in places Ananias' ministry was not going to reach. Ananias feared the Lord too much to allow another man's calling to hinder him. In my opinion, Ananias had the greater gift/calling and he should be our model in the church today. We do not all have the same ministry calling/s. Can I reveal what the Lord said about the people the two ministers were to give a word of the Lord to? The Lord revealed to me, the receivers of the word knew the ministers weren't going to give the word that was to be released over these individuals, thus the attitude of the receivers being the product of what was to be a blessing from the Lord. These prophets reasoned within themselves that they would deny a person a word from the Lord, because of a person's attitude. They used the person's attitude to justify their actions. There is nothing that you can do to justify disobeying God. Please note, it is usually the mindset of a narcissist/hypocrite to take something that is wrong, reason within themselves, make their wrong right to themselves, and use a specific thing to justify their actions. Believer beware!

The Keepers Don't Want You to Enter In. Why?

In the Holy scriptures, scribes were considered to be the masters of Hebraic law, even the writings they mastered through endless study. The scribes, in the holy text, were also referred to as lawyers. If we look at our lives and the things we diligently work toward and/or study, we begin to notice that through effort, repetition, and hours, we should master what we are diligently working on. These attributes should be a part of our daily lives. You don't desire to learn something and get worse at it as you increase your learning or study. The scribes in Jesus' day were keepers of the law, of scripture, yet, Jesus didn't just call them lawyers, He called them keepers of knowledge.

Knowledge: facts, information, and skill acquired by a person through experience or education; the theoretical or practical understanding of a subject

Knowledge in Hebrew: expertise, know-how, wisdom, prudence, insight, intelligence, enlightenment

Knowledge in Greek: cognition, awareness, cognizance, sense, lore, learning

Moreover, Jesus is outlining the scribe's ability to teach people their way out of bondage. The scribes had all the facts and skills to equip the children of Israel with knowledge, which in turn could have probably protected the region from the rule and reign of the Roman empire, in my opinion. With the scribes and Pharisees being the experts on the laws of God, they had the know-how, insight, and especially the enlightenment to set God's people on track according to the word of God. The scribes had specific leadership roles.

The Leadership

When in leadership, the main function of that leader is to help those that are under their leadership to come up the ranks, so to speak, passing along the knowledge and the tools needed to become successful as you work together daily, all to reach a specific goal. At times, there are people under those in leadership that may have firsthand knowledge of how the daily operations are to flow and can self-manage and may need little to no supervision at all. It is hard to lead a people that can govern themselves. People that can self-manage, in these settings, are usually leaders themselves, they just don't have the leadership title. In a business setting, managers love the one or two employees that can self-manage because they know they can count on them to do their job. There isn't a need to micro-manage there.

The scribes and Pharisees had a sense of leadership and power over the Jewish people. There are people in the world whom you cannot give absolute power because they are going to absolutely abuse that power. That power was keeping the Jewish people ignorant. This is why the children of Israel were not in a greater place of authority in the earth. Also, it was because of their disobedience to God. Now I get why the Lord says, His people perish for a lack of knowledge.

What was true with the scribes and Pharisees and is seen widely today also, is that those that are successful (in leadership positions) aren't really teaching other people to be successful in life. What is given is just enough to help you function, but not necessarily to succeed. I mean, step-by-step instructions, walking you through the steps individually. Why is that? Why are so many unwilling to help create more successful individuals that only lack the know-how? It is a deliberate attempt to keep the masses ignorant.

What I have learned from living in this earthly realm, is that there are many that do not want other people to possibly be more successful than they are. They are obsessed with titles, positions, degrees, and the ability to have the assurance within themselves that they are better because they have more knowledge, have more money and material things, and/or have more of a so-cial status/following than most. This is not just a world thing. This is happening in the church (the false church). Those in leadership are spiritually and physically hoard-ing what belongs to the people of God and placing in their own pockets, the keys that are to be used to ad-vance the kingdom of God, denying access to all except their elect/select few. This is not the will of God!

Kingdom Keys Over Prosperity Gospel

When Jesus preached the gospel to the poor, He knew His Word would bring clarity and a sobering of the mind. With enough of His Word being poured into His peo-ple, it will begin to diminish the poverty mindset that so plagues the poor. Preaching or teaching the gospel to the poor wasn't just a people being physically poor, but a people being poor in their thoughts/mindsets. Jesus wants our souls to prosper even as we prosper. In addi-tion, if our soul prospers, it is quite natural that our mind-set will prosper also. Jesus, Himself knows that not ev-eryone will walk in prosperity in our souls, thus He said the poor you will have with you always. Once again, not just the physically poor because there are many that are wealthy in the earth, but poor in their mindsets.

> "Beloved, I wish above all things that thou mayest prosper and be in health, even as thy soul prospereth."
> (3 John 1:2)

> " And be renewed in the spirit of your mind; And that ye put on the new man, which after God is created in righteousness and true holiness." (Ephesians 4:23-24)

The scribes and Pharisees had the key to this knowledge, the knowledge to teach people out of poor self-esteem, a low level of thinking, and keys on how to bless the Lord. The scribes and Pharisees were strict and very legalistic. They did not budge an inch when it came to the law and their man-made traditions. Everyone in the synagogue had to adhere to the scribes and Pharisees' strict guidelines according to the traditions of their fathers. If anyone was to deviate from those strict guidelines, that person would be deemed a demon. To a scribe and/or a Pharisee, everything done in God must line up with the traditions of the law and the traditions created by their fathers. Anyone that would cause a ripple within their religious views was immediately outcasted and assumed to be a misfit or rebel, just like they deemed Jesus to be.

What was Jesus desiring from the scribes and Pharisees concerning the children of Israel? What I personally want to know is, why were the scribes and Pharisees even around, and what real purpose did they serve? The scribes and Pharisees didn't cause a real change in the people. No one was revived, healed, or set free from what kept them bound. So, were they just religious police, policing the people of God? Jesus was in their presence healing the sick, casting out demons, and raising the dead. The scribes and Pharisees were with Jesus everywhere He performed a miracle, but watching Jesus do all these things, caused them to despise Him because what Jesus did, didn't look like their traditions or the law. They also envied Him because they could not do the things that He did (healing the sick and raising the dead etc.). Jesus believed, hearing their inner thoughts, and knowing their spirits/hearts, that they liked the celebrity of religion. They liked that everyone knew them. They wore very distinctive garb that made them stand out from everyone else. The scribes and Pharisees liked the respect and the prestige that came with their positions. The Pharisees were also lovers of money.

"Now the Pharisees, who were lovers of money, also heard all these things, and they derided Him. And He said to them, "You are those who justify yourselves before men, but God knows your hearts. For what is highly esteemed among men is an abomination in the sight of God." (Luke 16:14-15)

In a previous notation in this book, I noted that Jesus was prophesying about the church before it was ever created. Jesus told us why the keepers do not want you in the kingdom. The Pharisees were given the keys to money/wealth. Designated by God, they were the keys that unlocked wealth and put it into the hands of God's people, But they were lovers of money. In addition, it is easier to control an impoverished person and people that are impoverished in their thinking. With certain keys of the kingdom of God, comes the wisdom of God, whom Himself has manifold wisdom, which is endless. Meaning, God is wealthy and vastly knowledgeable about how He wants us to attain wealth in this lifetime.

Consequently, if the Pharisees are lovers of money, that means they want your money. We know that money isn't dropping out of the sky for anyone, and we must do something to get it. Most equate work with money, and it is fair to say that we want to be paid for our time. "Forget not His benefits", says the Word of God, pertaining to Himself, God is loaded with resources, benefits, income, and more to increase us, the church. God wants us taught how to attain the benefits of the kingdom through His Holy Spirit. If the Spirit of God teaches you about wealth, it is likely you will be a wonderful steward of His blessing. So, many of today's leaders start off well in the area of money. In the beginning, they seem to keep money in its proper place. Money is never before God. Then, something seems to shift in them, maybe it is the amount taken in that changes the leaders?

Yet, they won't teach you how to make money God's way. But they dangle the carrot of wealth in your face, knowing you desire financial freedom. Some in the church don't want you wealthy, so they are keeping the keys from you because it keeps you low and needy. They give you just enough knowledge to keep you coming back. Just like there are principles to salvation, there are principles to wealth and the Pharisees knew/know that. The number one principle of wealth is power. For example, wisdom is a principle that the Lord desires for us all, and power is a principle of wealth.

> "And you shall remember the LORD your God, for it is He who gives you power to get wealth, that He may establish His covenant which He swore to your fathers, as it is this day." (Deuteronomy 8:18)

So what is the source of the power? Holy Spirit. Holy Spirit is our power source to kingdom wealth. God said it will be done not by His power, not by His might, but by His Spirit. Why His Spirit? Because God's Spirit comes loaded with power and might as a package and so much more. We need to seek Holy Spirit for where the increase is because the Pharisees are not going to show you how to get wealth. Remember they possess the key to money, but they have perverted it because they love money above God.

Another principle is the glory of God. He has riches in glory. God's glory is wealth. There is splendor and brilliance all around His kingdom. The glory of God is luxurious. Why don't we see the glory and the fruit of it in the average giver? Why haven't we seen a harvest? Why aren't our seeds producing fruit? We are doing what is asked of us via the Word of God, where is our glory realm blessing? The Bible says the blessing of the Lord maketh rich and adds no sorrow.

> "The blessing of the LORD, it maketh rich, and he addeth no sorrow with it." (Proverbs 10:22)

The blessing principle is missing in my opinion. I believe it is locked up in the teaching. We must be taught the kingdom of God's principle of wealth or money.

The kingdom way of money keeps you aligned with Holy Spirit, not the world. God's wealth system involves purity, holiness, righteousness, and mostly faith. These dynamics guarantee we do not serve mammon. Mammon or money desires us to bow/serve it, worship it, and neglect God. There have been systems put in place within the kingdom of man designed to keep certain people out of wealth, but God will cause those systems to bow to His authority and His will for our lives. God's power will always override Satan's strongholds of financial bondage.

Therefore, there is no amount of fasting and there isn't some magical giving amount that we can give, and then suddenly here is wealth, no. God must release His power through His Spirit for us to receive His wealth. Holy Spirit will not release His wealth unless He can trust us with it. The best way to gauge trust is through obedience. Holy Spirit searches our hearts for obedience along with humility and being good stewards of even the smallest of things He provides. These are a few keys of the kingdom of heaven, to unlock God's abundance into our lives. Jesus, going to the cross-defeating Satan in the area of our rightful inheritance, is a knowledge key that has been suppressed from the body of Christ. These keys are now secured at the right hand of the Father, exactly where victory sits, in Jesus.

Satan gives his children money all the time, trying to make the children of God jealous and wanting what he gives his seed. Yet, we who believe Christ must remain obedient and kingdom of God focused. The bible tells us don't envy the prosperity of the wicked because it is baseless. Their wealth is rooted in their relationship with Satan which gives them a ticket to hell, if not repentant. I'd rather have Holy Spirit and be rich towards God than to lose my soul.

"Do not fret because of evildoers, Nor be envious of the workers of iniquity. Rest in the Lord, and wait patiently for Him; Do not fret because of him who prospers in his way, Because of the man who brings wicked schemes to pass." (Psalm 37:1,7)

"For what shall it profit a man, if he shall gain the whole world, and lose his own soul?" (Mark 8:36)

This Pharisee type of leadership today will be held accountable because they refuse to release the keys of the kingdom. The keys are not just for them and their family's blessing, Jesus called them "hypocrites!" Why do you think the top leaders that teach on prosperity gospel have renounced their previous teachings concerning the matter? Unfortunately, they still haven't released the kingdom key to unlocking your prosperity. To release a key of prosperity it is to be totally transparent with the people of God about money, not the false doctrine you taught for years. Ministry and money were never intended by God to be one-sided or flowing in one direction. The early apostles built the church correctly. No one lacked anything- in the first-century church. So many have preached on Ananias and Saphira for their disobedience with their money, lying to Holy Spirit about it, but cannot see the whole church of today lying to the Holy Spirit week after week, not providing for and blessing the body as it should.

The book of Leviticus tells us a priest of God has a duty to receive the offerings of the people of God. He or she must present them to God in a Holy manner. Historically, if you take a look back biblically, the priest always blessed the people of God, and outwardly expressed that blessing by speaking blessings over the people. Melchizedek (the first priest), who was the priest of God Most High blessed Abram:

> "Then Melchizedek king of Salem brought out bread and wine; he was the priest of God Most High. And he blessed him and said: "Blessed be Abram of God Most High, Possessor of heaven and earth; And blessed be God Most High, Who has delivered your enemies into your hand." And he gave him a tithe of all." (Genesis 14:18-20)

God gave Moses instructions to give to Aaron (the second priest), on how to give priestly blessings over the children of Israel:

> "And the LORD spoke to Moses, saying: "Speak to Aaron and his sons, saying, 'This is the way you shall bless the children of Israel. Say to them: "The LORD bless you and keep you; The LORD make His face shine upon you, And be gracious to you; The LORD lift up His countenance upon you, And give you peace." "So they shall put My name on the children of Israel, and I will bless them."
> (Numbers 6:22-27)

Just as God has given leaders the responsibility of our soul salvation, He calls for them to be responsible over our seeds in their ground and bless us as children of the Most High God and believers of Jesus Christ. If your seeds are not producing any fruit or you aren't seeing any growth in your walk as a believer, you may be placing your seeds into a ground of a Pharisee leader, that is not blessing you as they are required by God to do.

Jesus shows His disciples how to grow with little in the feeding of the multitude. Jesus took the little fish and bread and presented it to the Father and the Father blessed it and increased it significantly. Until the people in Jesus' presence were filled and had baskets of fragments of leftovers.

> "When it was evening, His disciples came to Him, saying, "This is a deserted place, and the hour is already late. Send the multitudes away, that they may go into the villages and buy themselves food." But Jesus said to them, "They do not need to go away. You give them something to eat." And they said to Him, "We have here only five loaves and two fish." He said, "Bring them here to Me." Then He commanded the multitudes to sit down on the grass. And He took the five loaves and the two fish, and looking up to heaven, He blessed and broke and gave the loaves to the disciples; and the disciples gave to the multitudes. So they all ate and were filled,

> and they took up twelve baskets full of the fragments that remained." (Matthew 14:15-20)

When Jesus told the disciples "You give them something to eat", He was giving them the example of what He has given them the power to do, feed them with the word "feed my sheep", as He told Peter, and by breaking and increasing the bread and fish, blessing those entrusted to you as leaders. Jesus is our Highest Priest and if He took on His duties as Priest seriously, why have today's leaders dropped the ball on this key of the kingdom and released increase and blessings over the multitude entrusted to them such as Jesus did, like Melchizedek over Abram, or like Aaron over the children of Israel? Is it ignorance? Could be, but shouldn't be, not if God called them into the office of leadership over His people. God fully equips those He calls. Once again something is missing, and it is once again safe to say, the church needs deliverance.

CHAPTER 10

THEY WILL MALIGN YOUR CHARACTER OR MINISTRY

You know deep within yourself that you are not what or who these false preachers are saying you are. But why are you disturbed by their erroneous comments? You received God's call before hearing the lies from false leaders. Why do you seem to doubt what God has said about you and your ministry? It was because these false leaders are well platformed, and have great followings, some in mega arenas in ministry. So, you want to trust those that minister to God's people. You want to trust their word because you see they have been in ministry for a while and God seems to be blessing their ministry. You are new to the walk, thinking they see something in you that you do not know is there. So, when they say all manner of evil about you, you begin to second guess, do I believe God and what He told me? These men and women are supposed to be men and women of God, good people, so you believe them because of their platforms or influence. It looks as if God is using them for the new believer. They will make you question if you are a witch, or a jezebel, or have you thinking, "do I have the spirit of rejection, or "is my character really jacked up?"

Could the new believer be caught in the middle of a psyops/psychological warfare? You, being spiritually immature is the only way those false leaders can get away with calling you what I like to call the classics. I've mentioned the classic insults before within this book. But again, these insults are the false leaders calling the true seers, prophets, evangelists, dream interpreters, those that receive visions from the Lord, etc., something that they are not. These are those that get labeled false prophets, witches, warlocks, rebels, arrogant, unteachable, and any despicable word they can find, just to undermine the power of God in your life, to get you confused and doubting who you are in Christ. Their ultimate desire is to taint your image so no one will hear you when you do speak the truth through Christ Jesus. I have heard, some have been falsely accused as molesters, or accused of going after married men and women within the church. Although these things do go on, these people were falsely accused. When you speak the truth of God's word, the false church will try and shut you down by any means necessary. The false church has no fear of God. It is horribly sad to hear these things about believers who honestly love God.

The false ministry personnel are manipulators and they do not want people like you and me in ministry for several reasons. They are scared that their platforms would be taken from them and placed in the care of true brethren in leadership, the remnant of God. Therefore, Satan is extremely insecure and so are his children. They are also weary of their financial security being stripped from them. Therefore, you will hear them telling the people they labeled to "stay in your lane." How could anyone say that when the only lane that we all should be in is doing God's will, and following the commission left in our possession by Jesus Christ Himself? Soul-winning, deliverance, and advancing the kingdom of God is my lane, not money grabbing, and butts-in-seats conferences. Apparently, those false leaders begin to believe they own the lane created by God. Some of these believe they have the power to shut you out. Thereby, believing they're shutting an imaginary door in your face. Not so! God will always make a way if you faint not and do not grow weary in well doing.

> "And let us not be weary in well doing: for in due season we shall reap, if we faint not." (Galatians 6:9)

In addition, this is the primary reason for the scripture that references *"the key of David"*(Isaiah 22:22). It gives the believer leverage against false doctrine and ministries. This behavior, "stay in your lane" shows the minute and low thought process of the church within the United States. There are too many souls on earth to worry if someone is coming after "your lane."

My attempt at showing examples of jezebel leaders and Saul-like ministries can become endless, but these individuals are working closely with Satan, some willingly and others unawares. But collectively with entities of darkness, those in positions of leadership honestly want to shut the voice of God out of our land. Holy Spirit revealed that when one of these false leaders in the church tries to destroy the character, influence, or reputation of another, they may get away with it for a time, but like everything the enemy does, there is an expiration date. Then the Lord of heaven's armies starts to fight for His Prophets, those that carry His voice within the earth. God starts taking the blinders off the eyes of those that cannot see who the true prophets are. While God is uncovering, He is also uprooting their lies.

It is a horrible experience to hear of these stories and fabrications leveled against those who passionately love Jesus Christ. Jesus taught us to pray for more laborers. When the laborers show up, the Saul's of the pulpit will throw spiritual javelins at their minds, having these future prophetical leaders running for their lives and looking for shelter in a cave. Jezebel is always looking for the mind of a real prophet, to snuff it out. Holy Spirit revealed that in the making of the true prophet, the lips of God are closely near to the ears of that prophet. And the ear of the prophet is closely near the lips of the Father. The job of a true prophet is to speak what he/she hears from the Lord.

A question for the novice believer, do you know whom God has called you to be yet? Why? This may be because, if you continue to give attention to the repeated echoes of a false leader concerning you and others, these words will begin to hurt you tremendously. As they should hurt. This is all a part of the call upon your life to release the greatest rewards in God. I can assure you Joseph was hurt when his brothers plotted against his destiny. I know it hurt again to get a taste of favor finally, then to have a woman accuse him of taking advantage of her. Joseph then gets locked up for her lies against him, which hurts. This is the time of your walk in God that those that lied, and those that sold you out, didn't know you were seeking the Lord the most you ever had in your life.

Focused on God

You were in His presence constantly. Holy Spirit began to put your eyes not on the things that hurt, but on Him. Holy Spirit's wisdom starts overtaking the situation and His guidance starts revealing who you are in the kingdom of God. I love how the bible never shows Joseph's hurtful moments. I often wondered why God would not allow for Joseph's hurt to be written. Unless he was a superhuman, we know he felt something. False accusations that put you in jail, come on, what human wouldn't feel anything? But the bible focused on the blessed areas of Joseph's life. It focused on his trust in God through the worst of times. It showed him staying steady in God. His mind remained sober and strong in those times, if not, becoming sharper.

Joseph's brothers were jealous of him. Joseph was already mantled to operate in many areas of his calling. Joseph didn't have a singular mantle; this was another cause of the jealousy. May I encourage you, to use the jealousy like Joseph did to shift your vision toward God? Do not remain in a place of hurt, if you do, the hurt will become anger, frustration, and impatience with God. And that was the plan of the enemy all along. Satan wants your vision obscured while Jesus wants the glory. Focus on giving Jesus the glory He desires. While the best way to get through the seasons of Saul, Jezebel, and jealous brethren in leadership, is through worship. It is trusting in God no matter what they say about you. This is what the Bible means by walking by faith and not by sight. Everything that Saul, Jezebel, and Jealous brethren present to you is walking by sight if you keep your focus there. But to walk by faith is your focus and vision pointed toward Jesus.

What did I do?

When deep down all you wanted was for the Lord to be glorified. I have gone through these experiences to gain knowledge of who I am in Jesus, to gain strength, and to increase my faith in Jesus. Do not stay hurt, learn why Jesus birthed you into this. For example, I do not know the entire outcome of this writing, yet I am encouraged that it may catch someone's attention that can make a change in the advancement of the kingdom of God in the earth. However, it is hard pressed to remove from one's conscience, when you see a scandal in the church almost every week. By now there should be order and discipline of the Spirit of holiness **(Romans 1:4)** in the followers of Christ. Yet, the church remains in constant attack mode against the authentic voices of God. But won't stop/say anything against those making a mockery of the church. I am reminded of the saying, "birds of a feather flock together." Maybe that is the issue here, false leadership protecting other false leadership in their networks.

When writing things of this magnitude that can possibly bring light to a dark area in certain sections of the body of Christ, one must wonder where has the fear of God gone? Has it left with this dispensation of grace? Grace is a wonderful blessing to have until you don't. I am afraid we have abandoned the true tenets of grace. One of the tenets of grace is the expression of God's love toward usward. Consequently, when God starts to expose these deceivers, mockers, and lovers of themselves, it will be nowhere for them to hide. They will not be allowed to hide behind their lies anymore.

For the fear of God is one of the seven Spirits of God and that Spirit is a serious characteristic of God that should never be played with. We show Him dishonor when we do not reverence Him from a place of leadership within the church, and it shows with the scandals that go on weekly in the church. The accountability of church leadership is at a higher cost than a pew member or sheep. We tend to forget the requirements to shepherd the people of God. The blood, not their blood, the sheep's blood will be on the hands of any shepherd that did not handle God's sheep according to God's will.

Bear with one another

Each believer has been assigned a unique task for the advancement of the kingdom of God. And I believe God places spiritual leaders in their positions for His reasoning. Also, my belief is that true spiritual leaders are to first bear with the people God trusted in that spiritual leaders care. The Bible tells us to bear with one another until that person is built up and mature spiritually. Consequently, this isn't a message to just everyday people dealing with their co-workers or bosses. This scripture is talking about ministry leadership and the pew members. Galatians 6:1 (KJV) says:

> "Brethren, if a man be overtaken in a fault, ye which are spiritual, restore such a one in the spirit of meekness: considering thyself, lest thou also be tempted. Bear ye one another's burdens, and so fulfil the law of Christ."
> (Galatians 6:1-2)

What is meekness?

Webster dictionary says meekness is: a mild, moderate, humble, or submissive quality

Synonyms: demureness, down to earth, humbleness, humility, lowliness, modesty

KJV dictionary definition: Meek

1. Mild of temper, soft, gentle; not easily provoked or irritated; yielding; given to forbearance under injuries

2. Meekness: softness of temper; mildness, gentleness

The Bible says we are to "restore such a one," the one who was overtaken by a fault. This scripture deserves unpacking because it is weighty. Who is at fault? According to Christ, we all are. We come short of the glory of God daily. Thus, we all have faults however, Holy Spirit is Spiritual. He bears with our faults even when man will not. Holy Spirit is the Highest of the spiritual organizational chain. Yet, this scripture is addressing ministry leadership while dealing with people possibly laterally or pew members.

What is a fault? Google says,

3. An unattractive or unsatisfactory feature, especially in a piece of work or in a person's character

4. Responsibility for an accident or misfortune

Webster says a fault is: weakness, failing, defect, mistake, blame, censure, err, vice,

We've all dealt with faults at certain times in our lives; however, the bible says those that are spiritual should help those who are not as spiritually mature as they are. These are those who have made a mistake or been blamed for an error. The weighty portion of the scripture comes with a question. The question is, what is the fault that is worth restoring through the spirit of meekness? Who is the honest measurer of the fault? I believe God places spiritual leaders in our lives for a reason. I also believe that true spiritual leaders that are founded in the love of Christ are to first bear with the people entrusted in their care. If entrusted, then that leader in ministry must be graced on how to handle people that are not spiritually mature, and that make mistakes that cause faults to occur. But they must be able to see the direction of the individuals entrusted to them by the Lord. The leader is called to feed (the Word), nurture (back to spiritual health), and raise them above the fault. I believe meekness is associated with longsuffering, thus bearing with one another. God gifts His leaders to deal with people in their care because it is a part of ministry, for the growth of His kingdom.

CHAPTER 11

WHO ARE THOSE DIVINELY IMPARTED?

The imparted are they who hear God and experience Him at a higher level. I know many do not believe there are those with a higher calling, which is partly true. Because even the greatest in the kingdom of God is the one who becomes the servant of men. Also, God has no favorites in His kingdom. So, you can say everything is sort of lateral in the kingdom, but the callings are definitely different. God distinguishes them and some are distinguished even before birth to set them apart from the world. Like Prophet Jeremiah, they are the individuals called before their birth. I mean those that God Himself has ordained before their arrival on earth. See, some people know God through a book and what their preachers teach them; that's a measure of blessing. But the few people that are especially called to ministry are those that had an encounter with God before they were formed in their mother's womb. Okay, this will get a little deep here, so I'm going to ask you to engage Holy Spirit with the testing of this next portion.

Some of the Lord's children can remember God giving them the ability to choose their parents. Some have had encouraging words spoken to them by God before they even reached the earth realm. These are those that know there is a God before they even step foot in a church in their youth. They are the ones who, "before I formed you in your mother's womb, I knew you" (Jeremiah 1:5). Some have sat in the heavenly council of God and received heavenly wisdom and mysteries before ever learning the world's formatted education. Many of you may be saying, what is this author talking about? I promise you; I did not receive this from a sci-fi movie. Most people forget this spiritual aspect of their lives because sin is designed to cause us to forget all portions of our spiritual memory. Just because God spoke to His chosen or elect before He formed them in their mother's womb, they still have to choose to serve God and His Son once born. If not, sin will continue to deaden the conversation, which if you hadn't gathered by now, is a spiritual conversation between God and the child before being formed in the mother's womb.

Here is an example: according to Genesis 2:16-17 God speaks to Adam about not eating from the tree of the knowledge of good and evil. If you notice, it was just Adam and God having that conversation prior to Eve being pulled from Adam's side. We progress to chapter 3, and we now notice that the serpent, being subtle, and conniving, speaks to the woman saying that she can eat of the tree. If we remember in Genesis 2:16-17, God was only speaking to Adam. So, how was it that in Genesis 3:3, Eve was able to give the serpent a rebuttal as he was tempting her to eat of the tree that God told Adam not to eat from? Eve exclaimed, "God has said, 'You shall not eat it nor shall you touch it, lest you die.'"

Here is a mystery! Adam, being a man, was made in God's image, the resemblance of Adam being pulled from God, paralleled the woman being pulled from Adam, meaning, before the fall Adam was the spiritual image of God and able to communicate with Him in the Spirit. Eve being in Adam spiritually, also received the knowledge of refraining from eating of the tree of knowledge of good and evil while not being formed from Adam at the time. Also, this signifies that everything that God downloaded into Adam spiritually, was also downloaded into Eve because she was in Adam spiritually. This is an example of receiving spiritual information and knowledge from God before being formed.

The serpent convinced Eve that the tree was good and both Adam and Eve ate of it. They did not die a physical death, however, they died to the connection of God in the Spirit, thus we lost our initial spiritual connection with God. This is one of the reasons for Jesus Christ, so we could get our spiritual connection back to the Father, reconciling us back through His Spirit. (2 Cor 5:18) God desires to have a relationship with us that is unhindered and having His Spirit within is the only way.

To some, what I am discussing here is quite vague, but to someone who has been imparted with divine wisdom on this matter, this is bringing the conversation you earlier had with God to your memory. No, you are not crazy because there are numerous people in the Bible whom God foreknew before they were ever formed or shaped. An angel came to Mary about Jesus, as well as her cousin Elizabeth about John the Baptist. They are the people whose mandate and purpose predate their birth. The words of God brought Spirit and Life to them.

They are the people God is about to release in this end time as well. They are those who cannot be derailed by money or fame because that isn't their goal.

These individuals have been divinely imparted by the Holy Spirit but remained unseen and unheard of and the false church wants to keep it that way, but God has an appointed time for their release, and He sends them to His assemblies. The false church can spot some of them from afar because when they show up, there is a power moving through the service like never before experienced, this atmosphere becomes charged and divine. And this type of atmosphere puts a halt to all the falsehoods temporarily occupying the position of truth. I have been blessed to see this.

I'm about to show you a secret that most of these divinely imparted and Spirit-filled individuals don't fully realize. The enemy and the false leaders the enemy is using know them. The enemy can see also, Jesus isn't the only one opening people's spiritual sight. Satan uses third eye, evil eye, crystals, bowls, mirrors/looking glasses, and star gazing to name a few.

Be informed, the enemy is always watching to see who is going to expose him. Satan is always scared of people who are like David, Elijah, John the Baptist, and the Paul's of any generation. Satan does not want the people designated to crush his head to accomplish their purpose without putting up a fight. Satan is swift in the act of deception. He has put blinders on the eyes of the people of the world to keep them blind to his tactics. Usually, he is the first to accuse people as false, witch, or Jezebel, being the accuser of the brethren that he is. Lying is so easy for the father of lies. He loves to muddy the waters so that people won't believe you as a person called by Christ; he wants them to assume you are the culprit.

The false church sees these individuals and starts attacking them almost immediately. Your first gathering with them (because of your ignorance of who you are in God because you are a babe) is smooth. They accept you because a fresh wind has just entered the room. The spiritually blind, deaf, and hypnotized cannot see, hear, or tell what's happening. So, you are cool to visit, as long as you don't try to interrupt the atmosphere of false ministry. They know those going in their service are gifted in deliverance and your presence represents deliverance.

The false church, the deceptive leaders, and the false prophets have been activated to oppose everything that is true and holy. They specialize in contentious environments. The moment you try to share the truth, they begin to form a web of lies to get you out of their presence, push you out of the church, and stop you from doing anything in the future. Once they design and start this cycle, they call all their false ministry cohorts and continue to spread the conspiracy. They begin to fabricate lies and spread rumors about you. They know you are a novice to things of the spirit, so they start the contention in hopes of keeping you blind to your call. Let this be said, you are not going to the church to take it over, but they will say you are, accusing you of trying to take over their ministry.

As I mentioned earlier, the devil has infiltrated church leadership through certain organizations. So, they know we have the divine backing and ability to usher in the kingdom of God on earth. Very soon, they will fizzle out, and the kingdom of God will manifest mightily on the earth. God is about to take their thumb off His called-out ones. It has been a plot of the enemy to keep individuals ignorant and deter the body of Christ from operating at its full strength – the greater works spoken of by Jesus Christ. Jesus declared the 'greater work mandate' to His disciples, yet I believe this is still for believers today. The devil and his agents are working tirelessly to keep the church and the people of God from doing the greater works.

> "Verily, verily, I say unto you, He that believeth on me, the works that I do shall he do also; and greater works than these shall he do; because I go unto my Father: (John. 14:12).

What are these greater works?

The great commission is foremost on this list. Jesus Christ ordained his disciples and, by extension, the body of Christ to herald the gospel of Jesus Christ. This command has not changed, and it is still relevant today. Additionally, laying hands on the sick and seeing them recover, restoring sight to the blind - spiritually and physically, restoring hearing to the deaf, and raising the dead back to life, are some of the greater works Jesus enjoined us to do. I believe the greater works are in the number of people commissioned by Holy Spirit to carry them out. Let me explain, Jesus was one man doing great works within the earth. Because of the Holy Spirit, there is a greater chance of doing the greater works in greater numbers. The only question is why aren't we doing them?

There is also greater work to do in governance across the world. Satan has infiltrated almost all global governments. Kingdom believers are supposed to be in government and in higher numbers than we currently have. As a matter of fact, we should be operating at a greater capacity in every system of this world. Kingdom believers must be present to shine as light in dark places of leadership and governance. Not just being there but making a true kingdom impact for God. Some call these the seven mountains of earthly influence. We as believers need to occupy them, immediately.

Whether the impact is natural or spiritual, it must start in the spiritual realm. I decree that God's light will overshadow the governments of this world. Whether Satan likes it or not, the kingdom of this world has become the kingdom of our Lord and of His Christ, and He shall reign forever and ever. These are the same kingdoms that Satan wanted Jesus to bow to him to attain. Those kingdoms were Jesus' anyway but because of the fall, Adam was stripped of his leadership of these kingdoms and Satan took over them. Satan still has them, but they ultimately belong to Jesus. So, our greater works shall be done in the kingdoms of the world, it is a must.

However, as I mentioned earlier, the devil has been working relentlessly to keep some of us blind, mute, and deaf. We must come out of this spiritual blockage to get busy with the greater works. The greater works (salvation, miracles, signs, and wonders) are manifested through us because we believe in Jesus Christ. The greater workers are to have churches that are actually houses of prayer, not profit or self-aggrandizement. Collectively in every sphere, we should be seeing the greater works. Satan has defeated us in this area. We are asked by Jesus to take up our cross daily, and that looks like doing the works daily. Because the church needs deliverance, she isn't functioning as her governing body within the earth. This life is actually backward, anytime the world is leading us, that is backward. The church has been given power to lead the world. The body of Christ has been neutralized, diluted, or power zapped.

Also, the greater workers build up the next-level leaders instead of holding them hostage on the pews. The greater workers ignite their communities to the extent that the unsaved run off the street and throng into the church, panting after God with the desire to know Christ. The full manifestation of greater works will make local hospitals call us to heal their patients. Morgues being empty, and police calling prophets and seers instead of psychics and witches to help with cases. Greater works are raising hundreds from the dead. Instead of the open-air demonic rituals like the one that took place at Astro world in November of 2021, where many lost their lives. The greater works are doing open-air healings, in the multitudes. Jesus fed the multitudes, and we have a blueprint of the open-air blessings. Satan is always trying to beat us to what we should be doing.

I pray we would have people in place who can heal the sick. The funeral home is calling us to raise the dead. How different will this world look if the church operates at its full capacity on earth? Yes! We have an active enemy to subdue, the accuser of the brethren is roaming our world and this must be addressed. Jesus has conquered Satan – he is a defeated foe.

Satan's jealousy and Fall

Let's start with Satan's original position. His previous position was that of an archangel; he was over the sound of heaven and a very beautiful creature. He was able to see a lot of the attributes of the Father (God). However, because he is the creature and not the Creator, Satan did not know everything about God. Satan will never know what the Potter knows; he is just a lump of clay.

Moreover, while serving in heaven, he occupied a sensitive office. I have heard people argue about Satan being an archangel of Jesus Christ. Let's just say Satan had significant influence in the heavenly realm. After the fall, one can still see how his influence spread worldwide. But he had his first form of influence when he was able to develop an insurrection in the heavenly realm. One-third of the host of heaven lined behind Satan.

I believe Satan was jealous of the influence of Jesus Christ in the heavenlies coupled with all the attention He was getting in worship. See, Lucifer oversaw music, and the order of worship was his primary duty. Note that the accolade of that worship eluded him, and it was directed to a more excellent deity, King Jesus. This reminds me of Cain and Abel; just like Cain, Lucifer became jealous; consequently, he led an insurrection. As well as murder, Jesus said Satan has been a murderer from the very beginning starting with Cain and escorted down the line to Judas. Truthfully, Satan started with Adam and Eve when he coerced them to eat from the tree of life.

God had all the worship, praise, attention, and higher influence. God's greatness displeased Lucifer, stirring him into a jealous rage against the kingdom of God, which is continuous until this very day. There is one entity that the gates of hell will not prevail against and that is the church. Moreover, he began to manipulate other angels against their Creator. Lucifer started to attempt to taint the image of God, telling the angels that "I should be like God, I am better than Him, I rule better than Him, you all should be worshipping me."

Satan was a master manipulator in the heavenlies, so what makes you think he would change here in the world? After creation, he craftily manipulated Adam and Eve out of their place into utter rebellion against God's ordinance. "For if you eat the fruit, you shall surely die" this was what God told Adam and Eve in the garden. But when Satan got into their heads, their spirit and soul were cut off from God. Satan performed this by twisting the word of God to cause them to second guess what

God said to them. And that is all Satan needs is a little wiggle room. Jesus gave him none, and Satan had to flee. Jesus fought back with the true word of God *(Luke 4:1-13).*

Howbeit, it was Jesus who laid down His life. To Satan and his cohorts, they thought they were just killing another prophet. But when Jesus hit hell, they knew they did not just murder a prophet. This death was different; it meant a change had come. The Bible records a great earthquake hit and the earth was darkened and the Roman guards knew then that Jesus was the Son of God.

When Jesus hit the scene in hell, I like to say that Jesus went into hell and turned the lights on. Jesus exposed every dark area that Satan placed in the hearts of men. Jesus went to hell and preached salvation. Hell was shaken, and when Jesus rose, He came out with people that got saved in and from hell. His light and power attracted hell-bound people, and they came out of the pit of hell free from the sin that placed them in bondage. This will never happen again, that is why it is imperative that we accept salvation now. Because once someone's soul and spirit enter hell, it is there for eternity. No one is offering salvation there. Salvation is right now! Give your life to Jesus.

In addition, Lucifer knew he was jealous of Jesus from the very beginning. Lucifer knew he did not have the power that Jesus possessed. That power is the Savior of the whole world. Satan is this world's deceiver and the blinder of minds. Now, Satan takes his jealousy of Jesus out on us (believers). Therefore, the church needs deliverance. We have allowed Satan to control us for too long through his jealousy of us and the kingdom of God we represent.

But how does Satan manipulate?

He does it by the influence he gained in heaven. Lucifer's jealousy of God caused one-third of the angels to turn against God, spurring them to leave their original estate, and separate themselves from their Creator. Think about it for a second, if Satan had that influence in heaven, what do you think he would do here being the ruler of this world? Imagine the tricks he would deploy on us in the earth?

We are not as close to the Father as the angels are, only because of our will. Yet, He is so ever mindful of us. Look at the strong manipulation that Lucifer has even to this day. Our ability to think isn't as enhanced as those in the heavenly realm, which is why we need the Holy Spirit. The Holy Spirit leads us to all truth if we are sensitive to Him. Holy Spirit is our teacher if we allow Him.

It is important to note that we are dealing with a master manipulator whose many children are wicked like him. Jesus told the Pharisees and Sadducees that they were of their father–the devil. So how does he manipulate? Satan manipulates by mimicking and mocking the kingdom of heaven. Similarly, to the kingdom of heaven, Satan requires human beings to advance his satanic missions. Satan must use people to get his work done here, just as God must use us to get His work or mission done here on earth.

Satan is the mastermind of all evils exhibited by people. He sneaks in unawares to exploit their vulnerabilities; only a few people can discern and halt his evil agenda. He craftily possesses the minds of people by attacking and polluting the mind. For instance, Judas was possessed by the devil to hatch an evil plan against his Lord and Master.

When Jesus had thus said, he was troubled in spirit, and testified, and said, Verily, verily, I say unto you, that one of you shall betray me. Then the disciples looked one on another, doubting of whom He spake. Now there was leaning on Jesus' bosom one of his disciples, whom Jesus loved. Simon Peter therefore beckoned to Him, that he should ask who it should be of whom He spake. He then lying on Jesus' breast saith unto him, Lord, who is it? Jesus answered, He it is, to whom I shall give a sop, when I have dipped it. And when he had dipped the sop, He gave it to Judas Iscariot, the son of Simon. And after the sop Satan entered into him. Then said Jesus unto him, that thou doest, do quickly (John. 13:21-27).

Satan has his own way of imparting into people; it is called sin. We were imparted at birth to sin, and there's no other way of encumbering you except at birth. This sinful world has initiated you into sin; until you decide to get saved, you cannot break free from its bondage. It is imperative to quickly make the decision to embrace Christ Jesus, the Savior, into your life. Otherwise, you will bear the weight of sin sooner or later. Sin comes with wages attached. The more you work in sin with no repentance, unfortunately, it pays out and the pay is death.

"For the wages of sin is death; but the gift of God is eternal life through Jesus Christ our Lord." (Romans 6:23)

Thank God for Jesus Christ who is our Savior!

CHURCH POLITICS

Carnality has continued to take a huge toll on the church and the operations of the church system. Over the years, we see how the church constantly tries to attune and adjust itself to meet the fast-paced demands of today's world keeping up with its trends. All to be perceived as "modern" or "seeker friendly," while producing a watered-down gospel.

These days, it is almost impossible to separate the church from the world; the dress, music, and lifestyles appear to be knitted into one. The church seems to endlessly borrow from the worldly archive of the cool and trendy or popular culture. Having a moral compass, accountability, and integrity can be an anchor for the body of Christ to remain healthy. In decades past, we have seen a world that had a better grasp on the above. But as the moral compass, accountability for one's actions, and integrity seem to be slipping away, we can recognize a similar occurrence in the church as well. The Bible calls it the great falling away.

Some people believe the great falling away is church based only. No, it is a falling away of the things that hold us all together morally. For example, we are in a time where society is trying to normalize adults being attracted to children, even minimizing the pedophilic label of these individuals as "minor-attracted persons." This screams moral decay. We are losing our grasp on our morality, accountability, and integrity. This is where the church should step in, in mass numbers. But you don't see them because even the church has fallen away and has been programmed by the world to accept immorality.

The church was constructed to help the world and be the world's moral compass. Yes, we are in the world, but we are not of it. But we are in it to make an impact in the world by being a light in the dark areas of our society. Unfortunately, the church has become weak and passive on issues concerning things like pedophilia, rape, sex trafficking, molestation, and abortion. This is another example of falling away.

Instead, the church is focused on one of many prevalent trends, that is the politics and dynamics of power that now play out in churches. The quest to dominate in a denomination and misguided hunger for power as expressed by some heads of church ministries and their board members, which could comprise of pastors, elders, deacons, deaconesses, or members of church statutory bodies, who continue to negate the plans of Christ for His body and tenets of scripture. So, now the church is operating and thus aligning with the world's governing and or business structures. Especially when unhealthy leadership is at play. This as well is a representation of the great falling away from God's original model and design for the church, which is highlighted in the book of Acts and the Ephesians 4 model.

Sometimes, this happens when heads of church ministries operate in such an autonomous system that allows them to rule with a self-governing hand. Their boards of trustees are carefully selected, yes-men who would never be able to put them in check or question their authority. Oftentimes, it is the absence of or partial obedience to divine instructions given by God through His servant that leads to some of the chaos and division we witness in the church today. With this knowledge, do we honestly think the church and or the body of Christ is functioning at its highest, most powerful, and holy level?

For instance, the heads of ministry leadership give instructions to the senior and lead pastors in the ministry, telling them exactly what they should do and how it should be done. But they, out of their own volition, choose to twist and tailor the message down to how it suits them. Thereby, ushering fragmented instructions to their congregations and pastorate. They are fond of flexing muscles and exerting authority on those directly under them. Choosing not to play by their rules becomes a real issue for any young and called-out minister.

Accountability

Brethren, it is quite unfortunate to watch the church of God, the dwelling place of God's power and the pillar of truth be in a place where cheap politics has become the order of the day. A place where men and women of God are seeking fame instead of glorifying the name of Jesus.

Don't get me wrong, I do believe in order, and like every organization, orderliness also is needed in the church setting. As a matter of fact, the church should be a model for order and sanctity.

Our God is a God of process, strategy, and order. This order is evident in the systematic account of creation and His patterns of dealing with His people throughout the scripture. There is a strong need for accountability when in leadership at the church level. It is imperative that we draw the informative conclusion that it is Holy Spirit that is our first and foremost Accountability Partner.

Without being submitted to Holy Spirit, this has caused some in ministry leadership to turn a blind eye to the multiple atrocities, or weekly scandals that take place in some churches, while many are not desiring to show accountability for how we handle the church. As leaders in the church, leaders must also have accountability partners along with leaning on Holy Spirit to assure that the church is flowing in the direction that the Lord is desiring it to. Accountability partners are those that hold church leadership accountable to the original intent and construct of the church. Also, they assist church leadership in keeping their moral compass and integrity intact. Our spiritual leaders should be gifted in this area because this is the basis of ministry after salvation. They cannot force you to have a moral compass or integrity of course, but it is something that should be taught, first. The church shouldn't be where confusion thrives or where everyone comes to give conflicting orders and exhibition of power; hence, the need for leadership and structure.

The first thing Jesus did when He was about to embark on ministry was to choose His twelve disciples. He could have chosen to bear the burden of ministry alone for the three and a half years of this journey, but He didn't. He chose the twelve. They were the people who followed him throughout His earthly ministry and kept up with His itinerary. They also learned the correct way to handle a ministry. They learned how to handle Jesus' people. They learned how to yield to Holy Spirit. They learned how to move only by the works that Father asked them to do.

More than being companions and learning from Him, they made His work easier. During crusades and teachings, they were the ones who informed Jesus of the demands of the crowd and maintained orderliness when necessary. Jesus taught them how to be leaders knowing He was going back to the Father. Jesus left them equipped and able to handle the things of this world and their adversary. If there was anything left undone, being filled with the Holy Spirit, the Holy Spirit would fill in the gaps. Honest question, is today's church doing the work they see the Father doing? Jesus said He couldn't do anything He didn't see our Father doing (John 5:19). Does the church even create disciples in the manner of Christ's ministry? The answer to these questions displays an error in our body thus displaying an error in the church.

Jesus the Godhead

Jesus is the head of the church and or the body of Christ, and I can guarantee you that the Head of the Godhead, isn't dysfunctional. There is nothing that is disconnected between the Father and our Savior Jesus Christ. Yet, the early Apostles recognized that their primary responsibility was to spread God's word through preaching, thus making the church healthy, seeing what they saw Jesus do. Seeing that they couldn't do everything at once, they created an avenue for the delegation of labor in order to thrive doing the business of the Father. They appointed the seven deacons of the early church (Acts 6:1-15), following the model set by Moses

(Ex. 18:25). They delegated authority to these selected deacons so that they could cater to the physical and spiritual needs of the people in the church.

One of the focal points of Matthew 21:12, where Jesus had to chase out the people in the temple, wasn't only because they were buying and selling, it was the noise, disarray, and disorderliness occasioned by their activities, thus, causing dysfunction in the house of prayer. However, it was at this point that Jesus saw leaders in His Father's house that were possessing unchecked authority and continued to demonstrate their lack of reverence by operating in false authority. This is happening in today's church, and when this occurs, the church begins to leave an aperture for the devil to penetrate and create a divide and rule the church system. A system where people only want to manifest themselves, giving little room for the expression and manifestation of the Holy Spirit.

The Bible recognizes the place of relationship, leadership, and spiritual covering. As a believer in God's word, I agree that structure is critical in ensuring the church is run in Godly order.

> Jeremiah 3:15: And I will give you shepherds according to my own heart, who will feed you with knowledge and doctrine.

Also, the book of 1 Timothy 2:1-4 also speaks on the place of leadership among the brethren.

> 1 Timothy 2:1-4: I exhort therefore, that, first of all, supplications, prayers, intercessions, and giving of thanks, be made for all men; For kings, and for all that are in authority; that we may lead a quiet and peaceable life in all godliness and honesty. For this is good and acceptable in the sight of God our Saviour.

Godly Leadership

Effective leadership is a powerful tool without such the church cannot run effectively the way God created it to run. No ministry can run without the basis of solid leadership. It is only a matter of time before confusion sets in; an efficient leadership structure is crucial. This is the solution to today's needs of the church. The church really needs deliverance in the area of leadership. Have you ever heard this saying, "It flows from the head down?" Dysfunction flows from the head down, but Jesus isn't dysfunctional in any way. Deliverance flows from the head down; Jesus is the head of deliverance. The church must connect back to its healthy head, its healthy leadership, which is God. Doing this, it will cause the church to move into its rightful status. The church's rightful status will be The Bride of Christ before Jesus comes back for her. I am just trying to implore you to yield to this now before forced or left behind.

Board of Trustees: A brief look

Although the position of the board of trustees isn't explicitly defined in the bible, it could be traced back to the early church, in Acts 6:1-7. Members of this board are selected members of the congregation who are well-grounded in the scriptures and have proven to possess great depth in the faith. They are the governing body of the church, saddled with the responsibility of fostering development and maintaining the seamless running of activities within the church. They perform legislative and judicial duties in the church. They also oversee the application of the bylaws within the confines of scripture.

They are the leaders in various departments of the church arm, working hand in hand with the leadership head. The board of trustees also ensures that the church stays true to its core mission and values. Summarily, they perform operational functions, which include church and financial budget oversight, performance evaluation and assessment of leaders, legal compliance, etc. However, in some ministries, that's not the totality of the board of trustees or governing body's responsibilities within the church, they do much more. It has become a platform where some men and women of God are victimized because they have refused to give in to unhealthy church board demands, following instructions that don't align with God's word.

Whenever I have the privilege to talk about some of the tendencies that go on with some church boards, it brings me to a heartfelt story that was narrated by a man of God who has gone on to be with the Lord. It is the story of how members of the board of trustees conspired against a founder of a church, to evict him from the church he founded on Christ. They said the man of God endured the days of their small beginnings and labored to gather men, women, and children in ones and twos until their population grew to about a thousand members. The church began to grow gradually and flourish exceedingly. And more people were joining in and pitching in to be a part of the congregation.

By and large, some trusted members were appointed when it was time to set up the church board. After a while, the church board members ganged up against the man of God and decided to kick him out. In no time, the man was gone. The vessel God decided to give the task of building, became a hindrance to the ungodly direction the church board wanted the church to now trend. It is deplorable to see the extent of man's greediness and how far humans can go to remove any perceived hindrances from their way, even if that person is the chosen vessel through which God gathered the congregation.

In case you are wondering, conspiracy in the church didn't just begin today. The power tussle between church leaders has been an endless battle since time immemorial. This mostly happens when we shift our focus from the very essence of our salvation, and we skew our concern to the cares of this world, covetousness, and pursuing mammon.

CHAPTER 13

FROM WHOM OR WHAT DOES THE CHURCH NEED DELIVERANCE FROM?

If you have paid attention up to this point in the book. You would recognize that there has been a common theme throughout. A theme that highlights a certain character within the church. I have made an effort to richly give a truly biblical understanding of the characters involved in church leadership that deals with God's people. Personally, when I read the Bible, God naturally highlights to me His leadership vs. the leadership that is on display in the church today. The two highlights do not match, which is difficult to say. Not every church leader is a bad leader scattering the flock of God, let's get that out of the way immediately.

As we look at the organism: (Google: something having many related parts that function together as a whole), called the church, we must first acknowledge that the church was established to function alive. Jesus created the church not just to be another worldly entity but a living organism that reflects humanity. How we see the church today isn't what Jesus intended when He left her in the hands of His disciples. The church is meant to live, move, and grow. Just like the earth was created by God to live, move, and grow. Such is true for humanity as well. God created three beings with the ability to live according to His voice of instruction, "Let there be." The church, being the last of the three to be created, just like man and the earth, the church is wanting to fall too. The great falling away that the bible speaks of isn't a falling away of people from God in totality as stated before. The falling away is the church system itself falling away from what God instituted it to be. Falling into the way of the world. Falling out of alignment with the Kingdom of God.

You may ask, how does something fall and remain at the same time? The answer is the expiration date for it hasn't come. All three organisms have a time marker in which the Father of all three will cleanse and purify what He created, and no one knows when that will be for all three, man earth, and the church.

The Church Oppressed

Can a living organism such as the church be oppressed by a demonic presence? That is an easy answer. If a man can be oppressed, and if the earth can be oppressed by demonic presences, then yes, the church can as well. Unfortunately, the church has become oppressed by demonic forces. To give clarity, some of the oppression that has plagued the church are the demonic forces such as the chameleon-like spirit, a masquerading spirit, and a projection demon. The demonic oppressor looks like he really wants to serve the true and living God. He projects the look of light from God. All the while oppressing the body of Christ.

Who is affected the most by this style of demonic oppression? Who has the greatest opportunity to succumb to this demon? To answer these questions, most of us automatically focus on those that are in the pews for the answer. Yet even that is the projection of the oppressing demonic force attacking the living organism, the church, at work. This demon loves to project that all the church issues stem from the pew. But just like a false light, Satan knows how to make things look a certain way. Let me give an example, which I believe we all can grasp. When you go to see a play or an opera. You notice a strong spotlight is given to those on the stage. But if you began to take your eyes away from where the spotlight is forcing you to look. You look around and you see darkness. You really can't make out the faces of the people around you. You can't really see what is going on within the darkness all around you.

The enemy does the same thing to us in the church. He loves highlighting the unsuspecting believer. Shining his false spotlight on someone in the church. All the while he is working his demonic assignments in the darkness all around those that are being falsely spotlighted. We all may be familiar with the scripture, "Satan comes as an angel of light." The difference between Satan's light and God's light is that Satan has a spotlight with dark areas all around it. Yet, God's light has full coverage, consuming up all darkness.

Satan hides in the shadows of his fake light working in his ways of oppression. Satan's ways of oppression are not always in the pew. The pew is attacked as if it is. However, Satan is using the pew as the scapegoat most times. When I read Micah 3 from The Living Bible translation, Holy Spirit leading me there, the first verse said, "the leaders are supposed to know right from wrong." And verse number two says, "instead the leaders are the very ones who hate good and love evil, you skin my people and strip them to the bone." Then verse three states, "you devour, then flog them, break their bones, and chop them up like meat for the cooking pot." Four says, "and then you plead with the Lord for His help in time of trouble." When I read Micah 3 and reflect on the theme of which this book is trending. I said, "Lord are You saying the church needs deliverance from its leadership?"

The Purification Lack

Of course, God isn't saying all in leadership needs deliverance. However, the Father wants the purification within leadership to happen first before anyone in church leadership can ever force the pew to purify themselves. Let's face it, the church leadership has not been honest with the body of Christ, by putting up this false perfection in front of the congregation, and not being transparent. I believe in encouragement; I believe that as a man thinketh so is he. Yet, we see a different story when we see the life of Job. I read the book of Job and noticed Job did complain, he questioned God. He did wonder where he went wrong. Job's life reminded me of a real-life human experience. I haven't heard many sermons on the righteous complaining of Job, God's perfect man. Job supplicating to God was Job's concern for the drastic turn his life went through instantly.

As I studied Job, the studies revealed that Job and God talked intelligently to one another. Job would voice his concerns and God would remind him of just how powerful a God He is. Job would then settle down for a moment and stir up again with a bout of complaining. Once more God would list His Holy resume of creation. Job pulled at God's intellect with his concerns. Unlike the children of Israel, grumbling and complaining as if God was not continuously good to them. The children of Israel didn't appreciate anything God did for them. Their grumbling and complaining was obviously different from Job's. Theirs kept them from the promised land for forty years. Yet, Job was more of an intellectual challenge posed to God. Later we find out that Job received double of what he lost because he remained righteous in God's sight.

However, I say all of this to mention that we need clarity in our warfare. What is meant is that we need to understand what we encounter spiritually and that it is okay to experience uncertainty. It's okay to question God, like God what is going on here? You might need to supplicate to God, cry out to Him, and ask Him the questions on your heart. Just don't stay there in uncertainty and complaining to God. God is perfecting those things that are concerning us, so He is willing to hear us commune with Him. This is another reason the church needs deliverance from the false and pseudo thinking that everything and every day is perfect or that if you are going through warfare, it must have been related to a sin that you committed or something that you've done, as Job's friends spoke, but was not the case. Job was a righteous man before God.

Blind Spiritual Warfare

Leadership in the church has done a disservice to some within their care, by not addressing the fact that there is a strong warfare that some in the body of Christ will experience. It's the lack of equipping the saints for that said warfare. Paul equipped his "spiritual children" with the ability to war a good warfare (1 Timothy1:18). Today's leaders sweep warfare under the rug, or treat it like it's the tooth fairy like it doesn't exist. The spirit realm is very real, and things don't just happen. There is a spiritual aspect to what goes on in the natural.

That is why Job complained because what he was experiencing in the natural portion of his life did not match his spiritual position with God. If Job's life was off spiritually, God would have never considered him. So, there was a mismatch of revelation going on in Job's life that he could not grab the concept of. How many can admit, your life doesn't reflect your prayer life for one, and two it doesn't match the relationship you have with God? If the answer is yes, always remember that God allowed it. While continuing to seek God just as Job did. Job had no one, even his friends turned on him saying he must have sinned for all this demise to come upon him. But that wasn't true, Job was a just and righteous man. It was just that Satan wanted a piece of him.

Just like Job's friend, I've seen some in church leadership try to make the pew feel as if their salvation isn't the same as theirs. I get it, there are rankings and callings in leadership within ministry. However, don't make those under your care feel less worthy or that they must have sinned or are still sinning. I've seen some in church leadership as well offer up this fake façade that if you are not getting the bag (money), then you are not saved and doing something wrong. They profess to know how to teach you how to get this dangling carrot of wealth or bag, but who and where is this knowledge coming from? And isn't it readily available to everyone in the kingdom of God?

In addition, when I think of the school of the prophets in the bible. The Bible never said the members of the school of the prophets paid to get knowledge from their leadership. Elijah told one under his tutelage, "it wasn't time to even receive gifts or money." So, you know Elijah did not require payment to be taught by him. The Lord revealed something to me via a question. He spoke to my spirit, He asked, "have you ever thought that the rich man in the bible that passed Lazarus the poor man every single day at the gate, had a nugget of knowledge that would have caused Lazarus to become self-sustaining and not a beggar?" I thought about the question and looked at the landscape of the current church system. As I thought about the question, I heard the Spirit of the Lord say with Lazarus and the rich man it wasn't about money. The rich man ended up in hell because he had what Lazarus needed to better his life and wouldn't share it. The rich man watched Lazarus day by day in need of knowledge and would not help him in any way (Luke 16:19-25).

No, you do not give everything to everyone because some will trample your pearls (wisdom and knowledge) underfoot like swine (Matthew 7:6). However, if God is showing you someone every day and you keep passing them by knowing you have one nugget that could catapult their lives for generations, and you do not do what God is so powerfully nudging you to do, then greed and pride have overtaken you (James 4:17). The rich man had pride about his riches and Lazarus had dogs to lick his wounds. The rich man would not even stop to help Lazarus. Even the dogs stopped to help him the best they knew how. At the end of life, both men were gone off the earth. Lazarus was hanging out in paradise with Abraham, and the wealthy man was in torment in hell looking at Abraham and Lazarus. The rich man began to beg Abraham to send for Lazarus to help him, but unfortunately, it was too late.

Free Wisdom

Did God Himself freely give wisdom or are we getting wisdom through another door, masquerading as if it is from holiness? Some of these false leaders in the church are getting information through a demonic source and stamping Jesus' name on it. I've often wondered how so many play on and with the name of Jesus. These are some either bold or ignorant individuals. It is apparently obvious now the church needs deliverance from false church leadership. There is a strong need for the purification process to begin at the head of the church body. Who oversees the cleansing necessary? If one looks at the landscape of ministry today, anyone can be a church leader with no vetting necessary. Unless it's you who carry the true anointing (just a sidebar rant), but it's for someone. God said, for those that the rant is for, He said "you are in the right place in Him, and do not let their false vetting of you thumb you down from advancing God's call on your life." But anyone can prop up a platform today and even garner a following with an influence.

Although, these are natural means they don't come down from above via the Father of lights. The Key of David in the Spirit opens the doors to ministry. As we remember from previous chapters the Pharisees and Sadducees obtained these keys. Yet, the bible never lends completely how these keys were obtained. But the Holy Spirit being the Spirit of Truth and a Teacher tells us that these false leaders got the keys to the kingdom through a false door (John 10:1-2). Moreover, these false leaders know the word of God in and out, and that is their key. Their heart was never for God nor His people. The Pharisees and Sadducees just liked the prestige of their titles. Like today, some church leaders only church because of the prestige Jesus' name brings them. Jesus warned His disciples of these types in ministries.

Jesus said, "they love the best seats."(Luke 11:43). In other words, they love the attention or fame of it all.

The Doctrine Needs Deliverance

Can we plug any of this understanding into any of today's ministries? I bet several of you can. False church leaders have gotten away with many false doctrines over the years. And a purification process has begun to crack through the darkness of false doctrine. If anything could come out of 2020, it revealed that somebody was lying and not hearing God as they proclaim. False prophecy cannot arise unless it has a false doctrine to stand on.

As information becomes more and more available to the believer, they are becoming students of the bible, just like the Bereans (Acts 17:10-11). But there are still some that are easily fooled by those that falsely teach it. False apostles and false prophets are on the rise and to be honest you really must have discernment to tell who serves God and who doesn't in these times, because many people call the name Jesus Christ and really don't believe in Him. They use the gifts given without repentance and fool a lot of people. The purification of God's church starts at His throne. He desires leadership of His house to align with Him in strategic doctrinal positioning. Teaching is so pivotal to the direction of the house of God. If the doctrine isn't true, then what is being built on that doctrine isn't true.

The Filtration System

Has anyone ever thought that if we all have the same Holy Spirit, Spirit of Truth, or Teacher, how is it we have so many doctrines and denominations? I have asked that question within. God responded to the question, His Spirit spoke within me and said, "My Spirit is the same and it never changes. My Spirit is the same Spirit that hovered over the face of the deep right before I created this earth. My Spirit is the same Spirit that raised Jesus from the dead in power. The difference comes because the filtration system in which my Spirit flows through is off." The wisdom of the Lord said, "the filtration system represents the mind." So the word of God which represents the Spirit of God goes through the filtration system of the mind and comes out differently. If the person in whom the Word of God flows through isn't purified by the Holy Spirit. Unfortunately, the spirit of the mind of that person will not be pure.

Seven billion people on the earth equate to seven billion filtration systems. Let's believe one percent of the seven billion filtration systems are church leadership. God said that out of that one percent more than half of them will not have the proper mindset needed to present a holy doctrine. We would not need all the denominations if we all had One Lord, one faith, one baptism, and One God and Father of all. One God/Spirit doesn't need multiple ways/denominations to get Himself to you.

It's our filtration system that fragments the faith. If things in the church were the way of God, the church would be experiencing the one accord Christian experience. The true church of God was never meant to have sects. It's the filtration system that puts up walls and boundaries which stop the pure flow of Holy Spirit.

If it's our mind that causes us to think we are teaching or doing church the right way, then one may say what is wrong with us? The answer is the lack of purification and sobriety of thought. The Spirit of the Living God isn't off. He occupies manifold wisdom. We are off, we are worldly, and our minds need purifying quickly. When was the last time you heard your ministry's church leader repent openly in front of you?

Even God said that He should repent because He made man. If God wants to repent for creating you, then how is it your church leader never does anything wrong? I've seen some in leadership caught in the act of sin and will not repent to those in their care. Don't even think they are going to sit down for a season. They keep going and their congregation keeps showing up. Jesus told some following Him to eat His flesh and drink His blood and many walked away from His ministry. Not with today's ministries. They do all kinds of craziness and people hypnotized by a name remain right there in the midst of it all. The filtration system is dirty and needs deliverance.

From whom or what does the church need deliverance?

1. False Doctrine.
2. False Prophesy.
3. False Apostles.
4. False leadership that really is for darkness.
5. Man-Made Traditions.
6. Lies.
7. Misrepresentation of the Kingdom of God.
8. Lying saying God said and He didn't.
9. Being messy/gossip.
10. Sexual sins.
11. Hatred for what is true.
12. Evil gatekeepers.

13. Those standing in the way of God.

14. Hirelings.

15. Greedy leaders using the church as a come up.

16. From the over-saturation of titles.

17. From those churches that do not reach out of the four walls of the church to help the community surrounding the church.

18. Man worship.

19. Money worship.

20. From the infiltration of Satan and the world.

God says the church must free itself from the soul ties it has with the world.

The Church Needs Deliverance.

CHAPTER 14

CHURCH FREEDOM

We know that 2 Corinthians 3:17 (NLT) says: "For the Lord is the Spirit, and wherever the Spirit of the Lord is, there is freedom." Don't allow the devil to yoke you in bondage. Some congregations lack freedom because the Spirit of God is absent in such gatherings. If you are a member of a church where there is no liberty of the Spirit, your spiritual impartation from various conferences and external teachings will never be received in your church. It is impossible to be imparted without aligning with the carrier of such anointing.

Orderliness is one of the major attitudes of the Holy Spirit, kingdom order, not man-made order that fits human agendas. God told me, "They will fight the spiritual freedom that's evident in you, but freedom is freely given by the Holy Spirit." No one should ever try to put their thumb on the Holy Spirit because that is a way to grieve Him.

Why this book at this time?

Jesus wants His church to be free and operate in power. He wants to set the captives free, give sight to the blind, and expose the antics of the false church system. Jesus Christ is ready to deliver His bride from this current malfunctioning model.

Personally, I have always had this burden and passion to see the church thrive on the earth and become so powerful that the gates of hell will not prevail against it. That is why God wouldn't allow me to be connected to certain churches or remain in an assembly where there is no free flow of His Spirit.

They are not obvious to the eyes, but there are demonic gatekeepers in the church who know all the true elect. Some church leaders are diabolical in nature, wanting to cut off the head of the John the Baptist types in the church, out of the church system altogether. John the Baptist's head was the target because the head is the epicenter of the body. By cutting off the head of God's messenger, one automatically takes off the mouth as well. While today's Jezebel-like leaders may not directly be asking for a cut-off head on a platter, like Herodias' daughter in (Matthew 14:6-12) asked of John the Baptist, however, they are using their power and influence to shut up God's true prophets. For those who don't understand this anomaly orchestrated by Satan, I pray for an in-depth understanding and lumination of the word.

Christians, beware! Modern-day Jezebels are on the pulpits. Many people call them Saul, but the Holy Spirit told me their personality is a replica of the biblical Jezebel. They fight the prophetic and do everything to hinder the obedience to God's instructions. They always want to be at the forefront of every activity, just to elevate their flesh and show off who they are. They try to silence every true prophet ordained by God because they believe God only speaks through them. They use their power, influence, connections, and status to get in the way and shut out God's prophets. This perfectly illustrates the Jezebel mandate – resisting God's move by polluting the land with idolatry and transgressions. Promoting the kingdom of darkness and extolling wickedness is the core assignment of Jezebel and her cohorts.

Nevertheless, these false leaders fail to understand that no matter how hard they try, God wants men and women who passionately pants after His heart to get His message across to His people. Regardless of satanic resistance, God's purposes will be accomplished.

Any diabolical leader who believes they can lie and stop the voice of God must understand that no mortal can mute his Creator. I am convinced beyond doubt that God is strengthening His prophets again this season, just as He did in the past to overthrow Jezebel's altar. There is an evolving revival; God shall again raise many Elijahs that shall utterly plunder and annihilate the altars of Jezebel's prophets. And this time, they will not run into caves, and Jehu will accompany them.

But before this happens, it is essential for some awakening and shaking up to first take place. Thus, the need for this writing. The remnant of God must wake up from their spiritual slumber and seek the face of God. It is not God's desire for His people to be ignorant of Satan's devices. God's utmost desire is to see His church operate in His kingdom authority.

Your Kingdom Come, and Your Will be Done on Earth as it is in Heaven

Seeing His church run by a pack of greedy and material-focused individuals bleeds God's heart. In contrast, it is His desire to see His kingdom come and His will done on earth (Matthew 6:10). This is exactly why Jesus drove moneychangers out of the Lord's house, and the true prophets of God must do the same. So let's emulate the Author and Finisher of our faith.

The real prophets have been hidden and prepared just for a season like this. They will come forth, and Jezebel will not be able to stop them. No longer are these pulpit-Jezebel's, going to prevent God's word from edifying the saints. God is exposing them as I write this message, and some will be gone by the time you get this book in your hands. When Jesus drove those traders out of the church, He said, "My Father's house will be a house of prayer." In other words, He was stating that no one would turn the Father's house into a money-making platform.

Dear Prophets, of the Living God, drive these imposters out of the house of God and take your rightful place in His kingdom. The Holy Spirit has given you the power to retrieve the house of prayer. They cannot harm you. You will run into webs of resistance, of course, but the Holy Spirit has gone before you, and His righteousness is your rear guard. Dear Prophets, this is what you have been imparted to do – restoring the kingdom order.

Dear Prophets, I urge you by the mercy of God, to be sober in the Holy Ghost when you are standing up for the kingdom of God. One of the reasons the church is in this precarious state is that so many prophets called to stand in the gap for the saints of God are not sober. Let the Holy Ghost lead and empower you on this journey.

Remember, the Disciples of Christ were powerless and fearful until the Holy Ghost came upon them. They feared so much for their lives that they didn't want to be associated publicly with Christ. The game-changer for them was the Holy Spirit. The power and backing of the Holy Spirit always makes the difference. Please, don't go if you haven't been empowered by the Spirit to do so. Don't go if you have not first gone through the proper consecration. It is easy to learn from the sons of Sceva that human motivation and determination are not enough. Subject yourself to the wisdom, knowledge, and power of God through His Holy Spirit.

> Acts 1:8: «And ye shall receive power, when the Holy Ghost is come upon you: and ye shall be witnesses unto me in Jerusalem and in all Judaea, and unto the uttermost part of the earth."

CONCLUSION

It was good that I suffered afflictions imposed by the fake church system. Yes, it's a pleasure because when you know God genuinely, and He knows you, there is nothing the corrupt system put on you that God Himself won't step in to eradicate. But, as for many others who have naively walked through this shady system and were steadfast in faith through it all, the affliction was for our betterment and for the body of Christ.

It's time to thank all who thought they rejected me or denounced my call. Yes, it hurt, and I am not ashamed to say their uncompassionate nature or evil affiliation did something to me. It affected my emotions because I was not ready for the high level of disrespect and lack of love I got after being activated. However, I went to Jesus Christ for my healing; He became a balm in Gilead for me. The balm that healed the wounds inflicted by those I thought were my brothers and sisters.

They left me in the pit and brought me out just to sell me off to foreigners. But God was always there for me at all times. It is amazing that the bible is silent about Joseph's mindset while going through his ordeals. God never told us how Joseph felt. I believe God did not say a word about Joseph's emotions because He knew we would have to walk through this with Him being our personal help.

Emotional tendencies may vary in this regard. So, God kept that as a personal secret between Him and Joseph. Just like all of us that navigated this season out. We cannot explain in totality how it feels, and guess what? God will not allow anyone to listen or help until He is ready to release you from the pit or prison.

So, to all the Josephs or whatever capacity God has called you to be, please remember that your walk with God may not be smooth – sailing against the tide after activation. But it will be for your growth and development; just hold on. Always bear in mind that God has sufficient power to make what was meant as evil against you work for your lifting. I think this is not just for you, but it may be to save other souls.

Finally, don't be angry, bitter, or become frustrated and allow the enemy to keep you from your purpose. Negative habits and/or negative thinking are a killer of purpose. No doubt, without the empowerment of the Holy Spirit, it would be difficult to forgive your abusers or shun vengeance. But one thing is sure, as you submit to the Holy Spirit, He will help and see you through.

Remain strong and stable, and you will soon realize that everything works together for the good of those that love God (Rom. 8:28).

I love you.

www.ingramcontent.com/pod-product-compliance
Lightning Source LLC
Chambersburg PA
CBHW050942050726
47592CB00007B/2398